I0504868

Catching Waves

Unveil the Secrets of High-Performing Stocks With Proven Momentum Trading Strategies

By Harvey Mcdaniel

© Copyright 2020 - All rights reserved.

The contents of this book may not be reproduced, duplicated, or transmitted without direct written permission from the author.

Under no circumstances will any legal responsibility or blame be held against the publisher for any reparation, damages, or monetary loss due to the information herein, either directly or indirectly.

Legal Notice:

This book is copyright protected. This is only for personal use. You cannot amend, distribute, sell, use, quote, or paraphrase any part of the content within this book without the consent of the author.

Disclaimer Notice:

Please note the information contained within this document is for educational and entertainment purposes only. Every attempt has been made to provide accurate, up to date, and reliable information. No warranties of any kind are expressed or implied. Readers acknowledge that the author is not engaging in the rendering of legal, financial, medical, or professional advice. The content of this book has been derived from various sources. Please consult a licensed professional before attempting any techniques outlined in this book.

By reading this document, the reader agrees that under no circumstances are the author responsible for any losses, direct or indirect, which are incurred as a result of the use of the information contained within this document, including, but not limited to, —errors, omissions, or inaccuracies.

Table of Contents

Introduction

Catching waves – The quick stock puzzle fixer!

Stock prices are generally known to move in spontaneous and corrective waves. Knowing the type of wave, and finding the specific direction or pattern helps to keep you winning and riding the wave of success.

While the stock market has served millions of investors over the years, it no longer denies that the term has been completely misused and yet misunderstood by millions of investors out there! This is because the past decade has witnessed continuous fluctuations in the stock market, with millions of investors losing out in the world of investment. The irony of it all is that most of these losses could have been easily avoided with the right strategies and techniques.

Most stock investors often think that investing in stocks is a simple method and a short cut to making a fast fortune. What a mistake! We've also heard about the countless examples of stock investors who lost vast amounts of money speculating in technology stocks, and other trendy stocks. Profitable and productive stock investing, like every other positive quest for wealth, requires hard work, dedication, and knowledge. It's not just a matter of buying into trends.

This book can prevent you from making the mistakes that millions of others have encountered while directing you to the right path to stock investing. Take some time to examine the content of this book, feed your mind with the elements and strategies we've discussed, and you will get to see how simple the stock investment world is.

I must say that it is quite an exciting act to share the experience, skills, and education I have gained over the last few years so that you can start earning like a stock investor guru. My record is as good as that of people who are considered as stock exchange experts. More specifically, I have decided to share the information contained in this book to help you to avoid mistakes that are common to most stock investors (some of which I have also made in the past!). The truth is - just like it is essential to understand some crucial steps that should be taken when investing in stocks, it is also necessary to figure out what not to do. The notable difference between success and failure or between gain and loss ultimately boils down to one word we've always been familiar with, and that word is 'knowledge.' You remember the saying, "Knowledge is power." Well, it certainly is. So here we go. Let me take you on a journey into the world of stock investing knowledge.

What You Should Expect in This Book

No doubt, investing in stocks is an excellent way to build your portfolio and, of course, one of the commonly used strategies for wealth creation. Hence, I have taken time to explain some essential trading strategies, one of which is: "momentum" - our focus in this book.

This book sets out a friendly approach to investing in Momentum Stocks with simple and proven trading strategies. The guide outlines proven stock investment ideas from the perspective of momentum trading.

The 1990s was one big roller coaster for most stock investors, with noticeable losses here and there. Well, the truth is that with just a little more information and a few strategies to retain money, a lot of stock investors could have hung on to their hard-earned stock market assets. The investment public somehow didn't avoid losing trillions in a significant stock market collapse. Unfortunately, even the so-called stock gurus, who understood the nitty-gritty of stocks, couldn't see the economic and political forces playing out on the market. Hopefully, this book should be able to provide you with a heads-up on those megatrends and occurrences that may influence the market and your investment in general.

This book is meant to provide the reader with a realistic strategy to make money on stocks. It describes and provides the essence of sound, practical stock investment strategies, as well as insights that have been tested over nearly a hundred years of stock market history. With the level of information displayed in this book, I recommend you take note of every strategy provided. This is to ensure that you get the best out of this book. Hence, treat yourself to reading the chapters in whatever order you choose but take notes where necessary.

'Catching waves' is quite different from most get-rich-quick books on stock trading. Instead of taking the usual outlook, I will be walking you through some proven strategies that can help you increase your portfolio. Why not let me take you on a journey into the world of stock investing? In a nutshell, you will learn the following as we progress:

- How to find the top-paying stock.

- Which stock you should avoid.

- When to take your profit.

- How to make the market work in your favor.

- How to reduce and mitigate risk.

- How to grow your portfolio smartly and efficiently and every other strategy that can help you increase your portfolio.

How This Book Is Structured

The book is detailed but yet laid out in a simple format. The sections are structured logically so that it can be easily understood. To proffer useful solutions to the problem outlined above, I have divided this book into three significant parts. This is where every other chapter will be drafted. This includes the following:

Part One: A Strong Base of Understanding

This section outlines the basics of stock investing. The ability to understand the essentials of stock investment and investment, in general, can go a long way toward managing your financial situation, especially in dire economic circumstances. We will be exploring the basics of stock investing in this section, outlining various trading strategies, and looking at some other essential concepts concerning stock investing. This segment explores some ideas that you need to kick start your career as a stock investor.

Part Two: High Performing Stocks

This section deals with the selection of good stocks through the use of microeconomics, which means that you need to look at the stocks of individual companies. Here you will need to use several resources to collect information regarding the current stocks you're interested in.

Luckily, we are living in the digital age, where information can easily be obtained. I will explain how to assess the essential variables that are tantamount to organizational growth so that you can decide whether a company is healthy or not.

So, in this section, I will be walking you through various resources where you can easily access information regarding different performing stocks you can invest in. I will also be walking you through the various aspect of fundamental and technical analysis in this section.

Part Three: Putting everything into Action

Here, I will wrap up the book with a step by step guide showing how to start investing in the stock market. This section puts every other step we've discussed in different sections into practice. Here, I will outline some essential strategies that should be taken to ensure you stay safe out there while increasing your portfolio.

Here we go, welcome to the significant work of stock investing!

Part One

A Strong Base of Understanding

Chapter One: Exploring the Nitty-Gritty of the Stock Market

Here is a quick fact - If you're not well acquainted with the essentials of the stock market, the stock trading details from CNBC or the business section of your favorite newspaper may appear to be gibberish. *This is quite understandable at this time of learning.*

Sayings like "earnings movers" and "implied volatility" are barely understood by an average investor. What then happens to new investors? I guess they'll be lost completely.

On the contrary, if you're considering a long term investment — with, say, a series of mutual funds targeted toward retirement — you may not need to think about what these words mean. You can do just fine without a lot of knowledge of the stock market. But *hey*, if you want to learn how to trade stocks, then you need to get your feet wet with all the information you can get on the basics of the 'stock market.' How about I walk you through the basics?

Origin and Definition of Stock Market

The term "stock market" is commonly used to refer to one of the stock market indexes, like the S&P 500, the NYSE, or, sometimes, the popular Dow Jones industrial averages. Since it is quite strenuous to monitor each stock, these indices are used to explain a segment of the stock market, so that their output is seen as a representative of the entire market.

In its simple meaning, we can look at the stock market as a market place where stock can be bought, sold, and traded on any business day. It's often referred to as the stock exchange, too. With the recent technological changes and advancement, it can be difficult for most investors to imagine a time when this term was nothing close to investing and trading stocks. But, of course, the whole concept of the stock market hasn't always been this way. There were several steps through which the road to our current stock exchange system evolved. You may well be amazed to learn that the very first stock market thrived for decades without a single stock being traded.

In the early days of its inception, the exchange was not the sophisticated global market that exists today. It was in Belgium that the first stock market was founded. This significant development happened in the early 1530s. Throughout this period, stocks were not bought or sold in the simultaneous global fashion that exists today, but instead, a meeting place between brokers and lenders was set up.

The first market initially operated without stock; the market at this point was simply a physical location where buyers and sellers or lenders and borrowers would come together to negotiate business transactions. In such a marketplace, trades discussed were primarily linked to government purchases, scheduled business transactions, and individual debt issues. Although many types of business-financial collaborations generated profits as stocks do, there was no formal share that changed hands in this period.

Where We Are

In 1773, the first London stock exchange was founded, just 19 years before the New York Stock Exchange was formed. While the London Stock Exchange (LSE) was constrained by the law restricting shares, the New York Stock Exchange since its inception has been involved in the exchange of stock in various ways and has since increased in popularity. Furthermore, NYSE was not the first stock market in the United States. The title belongs to the Philadelphia Stock Exchange, but the NYSE soon became the most potent and prominent stock exchange market among them all.

The New York Stock Exchange soon found its base on Wall Street, founded by traders under the expanding boughs of a buttonwood tree. The position of the exchange, more than anything else, contributed to the rapidly attained supremacy of the NYSE. It was at the center of all industries and trade entering and exiting the U.S., as well as the domestic base for most banks and big businesses. The New York Stock Exchange became a very wealthy company by specifying the listing standards while demanding transactional fees.

Since its inception, NYSE witnessed very little meaningful domestic competition. Its international influence rose in conjunction with the emerging American economy, and it soon became the world's most significant stock exchange. In the same period, the NYSE also had its share of ups and downs. From the Great Depression to the 1920 Wall Street attack, which left scars on the exchange— the 1920 invasion, was suspected of having been pulled out by anarchists, which left 38 dead and also literally scarred many of the iconic buildings on Wall Street. This literal scars on the exchange resulted in stricter requirements for listing and reporting. London, on the other hand, emerged as the regulated exchange for Europeans on the international level, this included companies that can list internationally. While several other nations, like Germany, the Netherlands, France, Switzerland, South Africa, etc., formed their stock exchanges, this development was only seen as a testing ground for inhabiting domestic companies until they made the jump into the LSE and the NYSE's big leagues. However, Due to weak listing rules and less strict government regulation, most of these international exchanges were still seen as dangerous territory.

Given the existence of stock markets in Chicago, Philadelphia, and other big cities in the world, the NYSE has been the most influential domestic and international stock exchange. Nevertheless, in 1971 an upstart emerged to challenge the supremacy of the NYSE – the NASDAQ. The NASDAQ, as it is commonly known, was the brainchild of the National Securities Dealers

Association (NASD), currently known as the Financial Industry Regulatory Authority (FINRA). It has been a different kind of stock exchange ever since its inception. As with 11 Wall Street, it barely occupies a physical space. Instead, it acts as a computer network that conducts electronic trades.

The creation of this electronic exchange made stock investing and exchange more effective and curtailed the distribution of bid-ask— a spread from which the NYSE could not benefit. This competitive edge displayed by NASDAQ forced the NYSE to adapt, both by listing themselves and by collaborating with the Euro next to construct the first trans-Atlantic marketplace. With this, investors could easily trade the stocks of various companies.

In essence, Stocks give you the flexibility of owning a share of a given public corporation. Thus, the price of each stock is usually based on the earnings of the corporation. In other words, if an organization's performance is good, or in some cases, if everybody assumes the business is going to do well, the price of such company stock will rise (we will explain more about this as we progress).

Understanding How Demand and Supply Affect Stock Prices

You must have read about and heard of a lot of theories about stock prices, their value, and why they randomly rise and fall; how profits affect stock prices, the economy, or credit markets. If all these variables are expressed in price changes, it can only have a minimal effect on prices. Nonetheless, those and many other variables change the supply and demand equilibrium, which is a fundamental aspect of stock investing.

The law of supply and demand is a concept that attempts to explain the link between a product's availability and the amount of its demand. Low availability and high demand usually increase a product price, and high supply and low demand lower its price.

The stock market may influence the price of a stock through the interplay of demand and supply. The price and quantity of stock where supply is equal are known as "Market Equilibrium," and a critical role of stock markets is to help facilitate this equilibrium. The law affects the price of a stock by regulating the prices of individual stocks that are displayed on the market. If a company detects low income, demand for its stock may fade, and the balance for both buyers and sellers is changed as the price drops. Buyers will start demanding discounts off the current price, and this will tempt many motivated sellers to get rid of their stocks. This creates more supply than demand when there are more sellers than buyers, so the price begins to fall.

The main drivers affecting stock demand are economic data, interest rate changes, and corporate outcomes. Economic data shows the state of the economy. For example, if the economy does better than the general expectations, this generates further stock demand in anticipation of better revenue.

Changes in interest rates, like increasing interest rates, tend to result in lower demand for stocks, as the risk-free return on investment increases. Also, when the economy booms, prices tend to rise, which increases the demand for stocks, so that these factors balance each other out.

On the other hand, a corporate outcome like profits, revenue, earnings and prospects of companies have a massive impact on the market for individual shares, accounting for the uncertainty that occurs before and after the quarter or yearly publication of their performance.

Companies may reduce their share supplies through share repurchases or delisting. This is when the companies buy their shares at market prices, sell those shares, and thereby decrease the total number of existing shares. This results in higher stock prices as long as stock demand does not decline. Delisting also occurs when a company files for bankruptcy or goes private. An organization may decide to increase its stock supply through initial public offerings, spinoffs, or new share issuance. Private corporations are listed publicly through initial public offerings. This gives them easy access to the public market. Whenever a new business is listed, it increases the number of stocks competing for the funds of an investor.

Spinoffs are quite similar to initial public offerings. Existing companies divest themselves of divisions that are becoming their independent firms. Lastly, businesses that are in serious debt may issue more stock shares. This leads to decreases in stock prices as the total share supply increases. ▢

Why Companies Sell Their Stock Shares

If a company wants to raise funds, they either borrow money or sell their stock. Each option has its underlying benefits and disadvantages. When a business owner decides to retain and limit the ownership of its business, the best choice might be to borrow funds. On the contrary, selling stock can reduce the ownership rights of a firm, but no repayments will be made to deplete future returns. Companies typically only list shares on the stock market once a specific size has been reached, and some industries never list them.

Generally, companies sell stocks to raise funds for investment. Stocks are partial ownership units in the company and have associated income (dividends) and valuation (stock price), which are one of several other options available to businesses for expansion and growth. To help you to understand this, I have outlined some primary reasons why organizations sell their stocks in the following point:

To Raise Funds: Generally, this is done through an initial public offering (IPOs). During the initial public offering, investors buy stocks, and a big fraction of the money goes straight to the enterprise.

On the contrary, if you decide to buy stock later, you will probably buy from another person rather than from the company, because at this point, they barely get any form of direct capital from higher stock prices. Hence, if people say that they are "investing" in a given business, product, or venture, we are far from the main story. You purchase an instrument that is usually linked to a successful business, and the company often pays you dividends. Still, your actual money is not put into the company; it is given to the person you bought the stock from (usually an exchange). This simply means that an organization can decide to sell their stock or go public to increase its capital base, which is often said to occur during the initial public offering (IPO).

A company that intends to pursue an IPO can go through an investment banker. At this stage, the organization's lawyers will send the documents required to carry out this process to the SEC

(Securities and Exchange Commission), and the brokers can generate signs of interest. The company can be listed on the stock exchange while the stock trades for anyone to buy or sell, specifically when the legal and contractual agreements binding the transaction have been met.

Generate Income for Private Property Owners: This is precisely how the likes of Bill Gates and Mark Zuckerberg operate. Once their company went public, they held a large portion of the shares of their own companies. Hence, as the stock prices of these firms increased, so did its net worth. Before they went public, their profit was only limited to the company profit, but after the listing, they now get all the money people are willing to pay to own a share of their business. Smaller firms are usually worth 5–10 times more, while bigger firms are worth more.

Public Awareness: Since stock investing is such an important subject and exciting topic, people think about it all the time. Thus, selling stocks is like an easy route to continually making news headlines.

Growth and Expansion: A publicly-listed corporation may require funds for further enlargement and earnings growth. If this occurs, the business can fall back on the market. The company must perform some legal and contractual agreements with the Securities and Exchange Commission, just like this is done during an initial public offering. The issued stock will keep trading on the stock exchange, but the new stock will not be available until the exchange commission gives the nod for the new stock. Whenever the new stock starts selling it generates extra money for the organization, but may as well reduce the mileage of the outstanding stock shares.

In summary, when a business is listed publicly, it becomes easier to raise capital. If the stock is a high-performing one, investors may decide to hold on to the stock. The strong stock market performance also enables the company to purchase other businesses with stock shares instead of the usual physical cash. It is important to note that Organizations listed on stock exchanges do so to raise funds and attract investors. However, once listed on a stock exchange, the company in question will no longer receive income streams from these sources unless it issues more stock. Stock exchange transactions are private, between the stock buyer and seller, and the company in question provides nothing.

Why People Buy Stock

I should probably consider changing this subtitle to "Why you should consider investing in stock!"

No doubt, the stock market has undergone its fair share of ups and downs, but in general, it has not changed the advantages of investing. What has improved — or what needs to be fixed — is the view of the stock market by the investing public, and, of course, its inherent risks. While you may consider saving a large sum of your money in the bank, you should also take time out to check out some reasons why stocks have remained the best investment and why you should invest in the stock market.

Attractive Returns: with the stock market currently yielding above 4.5pc, shares are attractive compared to many other revenue-producing assets, particularly given their intrinsic capital growth prospects. Return-wise, shares are considered to double or occasionally triple in relatively short time frames. Apart from that, returns of between 5pc and 25pc are a common phenomenon when trading performing stock shares.

Grow Your Income: Investing in stock is an easy way to grow your wealth, income, and portfolio. When you start investing in stocks to raise your wealth, you need to recognize that there is no given guarantee as to how your stocks are going to perform in the market. Nevertheless, to generate a decent return on your investment, it is not necessary to buy stock in the next Amazon or Apple. This is based on the instability of the stock market, their propensity to shift dramatically, resulting in a historic crash marked by a sudden double-digit decline in value from time to time.

Risk of Capital Loss: While a lot of investors with limited knowledge consider shares to be a risky endeavor, you already know that this is not entirely true. Risk becomes inevitable when you don't have the right information; the truth is, you can reduce risk if you are in full control and have a clear and accessible system of trading or investing in securities. Here is a quick illustration - flying a plane is dangerous if you're not a pilot, but this is a normal thing for a well-trained pilot.

Selling is one of the primary insurances against risk in stocks. When the market is behaving contrary to your expectations, you can simply get out at a predetermined price you've set out for yourself before buying the stock. For most people, they hold on to investments even if the price falls, hoping the market deities will reverse the trend in their direction. Hope is barely a strategy when trading stocks. Selling or reducing your losses, as they are commonly called in investment circles, can quickly help you cut unexpected risks. It also saves you from emotional turmoil.

Buyout Period: Many investments such as real estate can go on for months or years before a transaction is completed in terms of turnaround time. The paperwork involved in this process should not be neglected either. Saving deposits, unit trusts, and bonds may require a full maturity of at least one calendar year. But in most cases, profits can be realized with shares within a few days or months. This is particularly true when the market is cheery, and stock income often surges upward in cases when the market is characterized as bumpy.

Liquidity/Cash Flow: To sell out your shares, all you need to do is send in a sell order on the trading platform of your stockbroker. If the other side has an immediate buyer, the transactions are done instantly. There is no need for strenuous documentation and no web of middlemen involved. The good thing is that as long as you have an Internet connection, the transaction can be done from any part of the country. The money will be made available to you after a few days. This could take a shorter time in the future, specifically when trade settlement is operational at the NSE. This is precisely why stock investments are considered liquid. It only takes one transaction to turn them into currency.

Diversification of Portfolios: Stock investing is an easy way to spread your portfolio geared toward reducing future uncertainty. By including individual stocks, along with your bonds (and other fixed-income securities), CDs, and savings or money-market accounts, this will go a long way toward protecting you from the inevitable uncertainty of the financial markets. Whenever the stock market drops, the bond market moves upward. Hence, by dispersing your funds around, you can easily track uncertainty; in other words, don't put all of your money into just one type of investment.

Some Standard Stock Market Terms and Parameters

Before we go any further, we should explore some of the standard terms you will consistently meet in this book as we proceed. In essence, these terms are a must, as they can help you understand the essentials of your potential investment.

Stock Price: Stock price: The term stock price relates to the current market value for which a stock share is exchanged on the market. When its securities are sold, each publicly traded company receives a price—an assignment of its value that generally represents the value of the company. A stock's price may fluctuate with a myriad of factors, including changes in the economy as a whole, industrial changes, political events, war, and environmental changes.

Stock Volume: A stock volume in terms of stock trading on a stock exchange is simply defined as the number of shares that are transacted in a certain period. In simple terms, it refers to the number of shares sold or exchanged over a given period (usually daily). In other words, Volume is defined as the number of shares or contracts traded over a given time frame in a security or, in some cases, a whole market.⬜

Outstanding Shares: Outstanding shares refer to the stock of an organization that is currently held by all of its shareholders, including limited share blocks held by the officers and insiders of the company. You can find outstanding shares under the heading "Capital Stock" in a company's balance sheet. The amount of outstanding shares is often used in the calculation of essential metrics like the market capitalization of a company, as well as its cash flow per share (CFPS), and earnings per share (EPS). It is also essential to note that the number of outstanding shares in a company is not static and can vary significantly over a given period.

In summary, any registered shares owned or sold to investors or shareholders of a given company are known as outstanding shares. This does not include shares held by that corporation itself. For several reasons, outstanding shares of a company may vary significantly. If the company issues additional shares, the number will increase. Companies may issue shares when capital is raised via equity financing or when employee stock options (ESO) or other financial instruments are exercised. On the other hand, if the company buys back its shares under a share repurchase plan, the outstanding shares of a company will reduce.

Promoter Holding or Ownerships: This represents the proportion of shares held by a company's promoters. Community promoters are groups that have a substantial amount of influence on a corporation. They may also have a significant or perhaps a controlling stake in the company and may hold senior executive positions as well. Generally, most promoters hold close to 50% of a given stock to avoid any unplanned acquisition of a company by another entity.

Market Capitalization: Market capitalization refers to the total market value of the outstanding stock shares of a company in its dollar value. This is commonly referred to as "market cap," and it is calculated by multiplying the total number of outstanding shares in a company by a given share current market price. For example, a company with 1 million shares selling for $1000 each would have a 1 billion dollar market cap. As compared to using revenue or total asset estimates, the investment community utilizes this statistic to identify the size of the business. A company can be easily classified into big, mid, and small-cap companies using market capitalization (see chapter three).

Earnings Per Share (EPS): This essential financial parameter is often utilized when trading stock. It is simply used to measure an organization's level of profitability. Earnings per share (EPS) are estimated as the profit of a company divided by the outstanding shares of its common shares. The mantissa serves as a measurement of an organization's level of profitability. A company needs to document EPS, which is adjusted for exceptional items and possible dilution of earnings. That said, the higher the EPS of a company, the more profitable the organization.

Book Value: Book value is a primary metric used by investors to calculate the valuation of a stock. A firm's book value is the total value of its assets, excluding the outstanding liabilities of the company. You can easily access this information from the company's balance sheet. The balance sheet takes into account the accumulated depreciation of those assets. Simply put, an organization book value is the total value of a company asset that will be given to shareholders if an organization goes bankrupt and is liquidated. They are also known as the Net asset value.

An organization book value can be calculated as:

Book value = shareholders equity = Total assets – Liability

When expressed as book value per share, it is calculated as BVPS = Shareholder's equity/Total number of outstanding shares.

Dividends: Dividends are described as a payout by a company to its shareholders. Such payouts are usually made in cash. However, in some cases, businesses will offer stock dividends to investors, thus transferring additional shares to shareholders. This is commonly called stock splits. Depending on the time payment and announcement, dividends are either paid on an interim basis or final basis.

Deliverables: Generally, every publicly owned corporation is traded daily. In every traded Volume, a given amount of stock accounts for intraday trading. At the same time, the remaining shares are purchased by other investors for a holding period lower than the typical trading session. This, in its simplest terms, is known as taking delivery of the shares. In summary, deliverables are the percentage of this delivery volume to its total traded Volume. When deliverables increase with a stock price, it depicts demand from buyers, and vice versa.

This is calculated as the number of shares marked for delivery/ the total amount of traded stock.

Stock Chart: A stock chart is simply defined as the graphical representation of the stock price, and its movement between price and other parameters like time. Reading a stock chart helps you to outline the performance of stocks at different intervals. It also depicts the past performance of a stock over different time frames. There are various types of charts that are commonly utilized in an analysis or trading section. Some of them include bar charts, candlestick charts, and, in some cases, point and figure charts. More about this will be discussed in the technical analysis section of this book.

Market Indexes: The index is a single metric that depicts the value of a vast amount of stocks. Investors use this metric as a yardstick to monitor the general market (or segment) growth. The stock market indexes allow for easy selection of stocks. It dictates the performance of stocks so that investors can easily select a given corporation stock based on their performance. Stock market indexes are also traded in the form of futures and contracts, which are sold in any regulated exchanges. Some common stock market indexes you will see in this book as we may include the standard and poor's 500 averages (S&P 500), the NASDAQ composite index, and the financial times stock exchange.

The oldest stock market index is the Dow Jones Industrial Average (DJIA or "The Dow"). In 1896, Charles Dow (of the renown of Dow Jones) produced the Dow Jones Industrial Average; at that time, it included just 12 stocks (the number increased to 30 in 1928 and has remained the same to this day).

Chapter Two: The Upward, Downward, And Side-Way Spiral

A quick fact - there is no magic formula for predicting the stock market. Several issues affect share price ebbs and flows, whether subtle changes or sudden spikes. Hence, you may need to get your hands wet with various strategies to improve the odds in your favor. Well, the stock market direction is just another strategy that can be used to twist market behavior to your advantage. It is one of the most critical components of stock trading and investment.

I will be addressing stock market directions in this chapter, which will serve as a guideline in determining which stocks to buy and when, while maintaining track of ups and downswings over individual stock history.

Exploring Market Jargon

Before we go any further, let's take a look at some market jargon essential to this section.

Tops or Peaks: We often visualize a 'mountain' when we think of the term 'peaks' or 'tops.' Similarly, when looking at a stock map, it is easy to perceive the notable signs of mountains and hilly shapes. Even in investment terms, the edges of these notable hilly shapes are called "tops." Just like the peak of a 'mountain' is known as its extreme point, the same term is also applicable to the investment world. Thus, the extreme or highest point of a stock is known as a 'stock price top.'

Bottoms and Troughs: when we change the direction of a mountain, we have a trough or a valley. And just like the name implies, it's the lowest point on the ground. In the same way, the stock charts have a' bottom' or' trough' – this is known as the smallest price a stock dropped to.

What is the Market Direction?

As discussed in the previous section, stock prices are usually volatile. They barely move in a predefined direction. A stock market direction is the general tendency of the stock markets to move with a specific trend over a given period. They are often called market trends by most investment and financial analysts.

These directions are categorized as secular movements for a more extended period, primary for moderate time scales, and secondary for shorter time scales. You can easily define market trends through technical analysis (see chapter nine), a framework that characterizes market directions as likely market price trends when prices reach specific support levels, which varies with time.

In general, the sideways, upward, or downward movement of the stock price over time is known as a market direction or trend. In simple terms, an upward movement of the stock market is called an uptrend, while those that move downward, usually in descending order over time, are said to be a downtrend. A sideways movement, on the other hand, is the horizontal price shift that happens when the effects of supply and demand are almost balanced. This is usually the case during the restructuring phase until a previous trend continues or a new trend is reversed. A sideways market direction is commonly referred to as the "horizontal trend."

Every rational investor is expected to sell stocks that are moving in a downward trend, while stocks that are moving upwards are purchased.

But then, stock prices are generally known to move in zigzags. In technical analysis, we may not define a market direction based on how far up or down the price of the Stock has been driven over a given period. Instead, we're concerned about the details; that is, the extent to which the stock price is increasing over time, or how little it has dropped in a downward direction.

How Market Trends Work

The Uptrend: During an uptrend, the tops and bottoms of the stock chart are seen growing progressively. Therefore, the price of a given stock comes to a different peak and drops below what it was.

Don't get me wrong; this does not mean that the stock price will record a new high in its life span. This new high may only persist for a few days, weeks, or months. However, this steady increase in the peaks and troughs shows that the value of the stock is increasing. In other words, the Stock may have a tendency to increase in value rather than depreciating. Therefore, traders can buy more in cases like this, rather than selling stock. This can, in turn, result in a tremendous increase in the price of stocks.

More than this, any time a stock falls, buyers believe it is the right time to buy more stocks. They barely wait for a reduction in its price level.

This tends to halt any potential decrease in the price of the stock.

The Downtrend: A downtrend is a trend in which stocks drop continuously. In this case, successive peaks and troughs become lower. This implies that market participants are confident that the Stock will fall lower. Hence, a small increase in the price of stocks serves as an opportunity for a quick sell-off. Buying these stocks during this period is often difficult. Such a stock cannot be traded, no matter how much the price has dropped— particularly true when you are a quick-term (short term) stock trader.

Sideways/Horizontal Trend: For a sideways movement, the Stock does not shift in either an upward or a downward direction. Tops and bottoms remain constant over time, with no specific direction to indicate whether to buy a stock, or sell-off a stock.

No doubt, the best thing happens only by using patience and determination. The first logical step for any student of technical analysis should be to understand how to define the market direction. For most investors, once they have invested in the uptrend, they will remain there searching for any weakness in the uptrend, which they see as a signal required for hopping out and making a considerable profit.

We must elaborate more on market direction, using the various categorizations of market directions/trends.

Secular Trends, Market, and Stock

Secular is a general term used to define long-term business practices. Secular can also be used to refer to specific stocks that are not affected by brief trends. They are neither seasonal nor cyclical. Alternatively, they stay consistent over the years. Secular stocks retain a static path, irrespective of present economic trends and conditions. By applying this word to the stock market, the secular market or trend can be used to explain trends that are persistent for more than five years. Therefore, structural movements of these trends may be in an uptrend or a downtrend.

A secular trend is a market trend that can last for one to three decades. It has many critical patterns within its boundaries, and for the most part, it is easy to spot because of the long time frame. Here, stock market participants expect this trend to continue moving toward an identical direction, and over a longer period. Stocks become secular when a given company's earnings remain constant, irrespective of several other changes in the market. Industries are often secular when an organization's core business involves consumer staples or items that are commonly used by most individuals.

A secular trend can depict either a negative or a positive movement. Consequently, the concept does not only imply advancement or growth. In other words, a secular trend can depict a reduction or an expansion. Also, secular in this term can refer to precise or intense change, as the term does not indicate the precise level of change. The distinctive hallmarks here are the long-term essence of the phenomenon and the low impact on the related development of short-term movements. While secular trends are far from our main focus in this book, you must recognize the impacts of secular market trends as an investor. This is particularly important if you are looking to establish a long-term trading strategy for the future. A quick illustration of secular patterns or trends may include the aging population, which continues to have distinct spending and saving patterns as differing from the younger age groups, the proliferation of innovation, and the heavy dependency on some resources like oil. However, while analysts believe secular trends to be long-term trends or strategies, secular patterns are not constant.

Primary Market Trends

A primary market is an accumulated period in a market cycle during which stock prices continue to rise (bull market) or fall (bear market) before peaking and reversal while establishing a trend in a reverse direction. The primary trend may last up to two years and comprises of a set of secondary market trends. Hence, the bull and bear market are known as primary markets.

No one knows the exact roots of the words "bull" and "bear" in the definition as used by the stock market, but their meanings are fairly clear. A significant thing to note about these concepts is that they reflect long-term patterns and not short-term shifts. Bull and bear markets are typically measured over the years.

The bull market is a growing market. Investors are usually optimistic in the bull market. Here, the economy appears to be good, the unemployment rate is low, and end-users spend more money, which generally increases an organization's revenue. As businesses make profits, investors may decide to share a slice of the cake — hence, they purchase stocks and relax and watch the cash roll in. The supply of shares at this point becomes low — so that nobody gives up their slice of the cake. The rivalry to purchase those much-loved shares is becoming intense, which may drive stock prices up even higher. Investors are taking risks because they feel optimistic about their chance of earning serious cash.

On the other hand, the bear market is a declining market. It often begins with a rapid decline in stock prices over time. There is generally an eye to the storm, in which stock prices are rising. But the storm is coming back, of course, and the bear market is dropping fast. Particularly bloodthirsty bears, like the one that destroyed the United States during the Great Depression, could result in prices being about 90 percent lower than normal, and the economy is poor. Unemployment rises, and consumers spend less, resulting in lower business profits. As we have seen, this devalues the company in question.

Riding the Bull and Taming the Bear

The best strategy to make money in a bull market is to identify the movement early and make smart purchases. Ever heard of buying low and selling high? It may seem contrary-intuitive that you can earn money in a bear market, but here are a few guides to keep you informed on how you can tame a bear before you dive deeper.

- **Short Selling**: this may require extensive skill on the part of the investor. Short selling is a trade that consists of having to borrow stock that you don't own, selling it, waiting for the prices to fall, then purchasing it back at a lower price, and thus earning a return on investment.

- **Defensive Stocks**: this is a minimal-risk way for stock traders to hold their money in the stock market. It is often called defensive stock because its value does not vary immensely. Utility stocks (energy, water, etc.) are typical examples of defensive stocks.

Secondary Trends

Secondary trends are defined as short-term alterations or movement in price that occur in a primary trend. Just like the name implies, they occur in the short-term. Hence, they may only persist for a couple of months, and in some cases, weeks. For a better understanding, we will explain them in the following terms below:

Market Corrections: in many cases, a brief change or movement in price can be called a market correction. This correction is a quick-term price reduction of 5% to 20% or thereabouts.

An example can be seen by looking at a situation ten years ago in April when the S&P index dropped from 1,300 to nearly 1,000. To many, it was regarded as the close of the bullish market and the beginning of the bearish market. But in real terms, it was far from it, as the market made a turnaround. In a simple definition, a market correction is a bullish momentum that is barely sufficient to be a market for bears.

Sucker Rally: The sucker rally, popularly known as the "bear market rally," is a price hike of 10% to 20% or more before prices recede again. The sucker rally occurred in the Dow Jones Index following the Wall Street Crash in the year 1929, which led to a downside in the market during the 1930s and throughout the late '60s and early '70s.

The price of securities, like stocks, is determined by the free interplay of demand and supply. In nature, the market combines the activities of stock dealers, which makes it difficult to have more buyers of stock than sellers or the reverse. In the event of a rise in prices, the buyers may increase the amount they can pay. In contrast, the sellers increase the amount they are willing to take. When there is a boom in production, the reverse occurs.

Demand and supply vary significantly as market participants try to change the distribution of their investments between types of assets. For instance, at some point, traders may want to transfer money from bonds to "internet" stocks, but they can only thrive if someone else is prepared to purchase the bonds they are offering for sale. In some cases, they may attempt to move money from a given stock say, "internet" stocks, to bonds. In these scenarios, this will have an impact on the price of each type of security.

Theoretically, market participants will want to time the market when buying low and selling high, but they often end up doing the opposite. Contrarian market participants are attempting to "fade" investors' behavior by selling when investors are buying and buying when they are selling. The period when most stock traders sell securities like stock is referred to as 'distribution.' On the contrary, when so many investors buy shares, we call it accumulation.

As shown by standard theory, lower prices would lead to more demand and lower supply of stocks, whereas a price increase will do the reverse. This analysis may work correctly for most commodities but often functions inversely for stocks owing to the fallacy many investors are believed to make when they buy high in anxiety and sell low in panic. If a rise in prices leads to high demand or a reduction in prices results in increased supply, it eliminates the predicted vicious cycle, and markets will be far from stable. This can be referred to as a market bubble.

In summary, the stock market is comprised of various types of trends, and understanding these trends will largely determine the success of your long term and short-term stock investments (and specifically for stock investors who are momentum traders).

Ideally, market directions/trends provide the basics from which technical analysis is performed. The information provided is aimed toward giving you a fundamental understanding of how the market performs so that you can easily make sense out of the market when performing technical analysis.

Chapter Three: Who Will Win The Race, Small, Mid, or the Big *'Cap'* Company?

The size of every company is another essential concept that you need to understand when acquiring stocks or assets. Companies are classified into small, medium, and large-cap categories to help you quickly understand the size of the business you wish to invest in. This section outlines various types of market capitalization.

Exploring the Basics

It's easy to identify a stock price, but perhaps, the new trading price of a stock doesn't say a lot about the value of a stock, business, or company. Share prices may stay above $1 per share in stock exchanges and can quickly grow to hundreds or thousands of dollars per share.

The popularly known 'cap' you've probably heard about in stock investing like small-cap, mid-cap, and large-cap, refers to the market capitalization of a business. Market capitalization, as popularly called the market cap by most investment gurus, is computed by multiplying the outstanding shares of the company by its share price. It serves as an easy way to determine the size of a company. In essence, the stock price of a corporation alone does not say much about the size of the business. For example, a corporation with a stock quote of $50 is not particularly more valuable than a company with a stock quote of $20. using a simple analysis, a corporation with a stock quote of $50 and a hundred million shares outstanding (a market cap of $5 billion) is lower in value than that of a corporation with a stock quote of $20 and five hundred million shares outstanding (a market cap of $10 billion).

Outstanding Stock vs. Float Stock vs. Restricted Stock

The outstanding shares of a company are comprised of float and restricted stock. Outstanding shares, as we already know, refer to the shares (issued shares) owned in the public domain by investors, management of the company, and shareholders. Outstanding stocks, however, do not include treasury stock. On the other hand, the term "float stock" refers to the shares of a company that were issued to the public and are available to stock traders to trade in the stock market. Stock data like the number of shares issued and "float," indicates the company's market perception.

Floating stock is determined by deducting close-held securities from the total outstanding shares of a company and restricted stock. Shares that are closely held are those stocks that are owned by organization executives, major shareholders, and employees. Restricted stock, on the other hand, refers to insider shares that cannot be traded after an initial public offering, which is usually due to a temporary restriction such as the lock-up period.

In general, stocks with a small float are generally considered to be more unstable than a stock with a full float. This is because it may be challenging to find a buyer or seller when restricted shares are available. This leads to lower volume and broader spreads.

Free-Float Weighting

Free-float weighting is a popular form of capitalization weighting. Here, a float variable is applied to each share to compensate for the percentage of outstanding shares purchased by the public, contrary to "closely held" shares that are owned by the government, shareholders, or insiders within a given corporation. For instance, if 10 percent of the shares are owned tightly and the other 90 percent are held publicly, the float variable will be 0.90, through which the market capitalization of the corporation will be weighted before weighting its value against all other indexes. The amount of shares used for this estimation is the number of stocks that are "floating" rather than just outstanding.

An important index that is weighted in this way is called "float-adjusted" or "float-weighted." For instance, the S&P 500 index is both float-adjusted and cap-weighted.

Publicly listed firms are usually classified into three distinct categories of market caps: large-caps, medium (mid) caps, and small-caps. Categorizations may differ; that is, not everyone accepts the same market cap cuts for each category, but the classes are sometimes described and defined as below.

The Small-Cap Company

Usually, small-cap companies are classified as corporations with a market capitalization below $2 billion. Most small-cap companies are new companies still at their early stages of development with a significant potential for growth. However, the level of risk and failure is usually higher for small-cap stocks when compared to the mid-cap and large-cap stocks. Hence, they are often considered to be more uncertain than both big-cap and medium-cap companies and stocks. In fact, small-cap companies throughout economic downturns generally perform poorly rather than large-cap companies who perform well. Still, in most cases, they record tremendous performance when compared to large-cap companies as the economy recovers from economic downturns.

The small stocks of small-cap companies are often referred to as nano-cap stocks and micro-cap stocks. Micro-cap stocks may fall between $50 million and $2 billion in market cap. In contrast, nano-cap stocks are quite small and may fall below $50 million, and are considered more hazardous than small-cap stocks. Although the potential for these businesses to achieve rapid growth is fantastic, it's also possible that you may risk a great deal of money.

The Mid-Cap Company

Mid-caps are generally defined as organizations with market caps that are around $2 billion and $10 billion. Mid-cap stocks seem to be more volatile than stocks on large-cap but less volatile than stocks on small-cap. Nonetheless, mid-cap stocks tend to offer more potential for growth than big-cap stocks.

The Large-Cap Company

Large-caps are commonly defined as corporations with market caps amounting to or above $10 billion. Mega caps are also included within large-caps and are widely characterized as corporations with market caps of $200 billion or higher. Such corporations are regarded as stable organizations that have market dominance within their specific industries. Wal-Mart, one of the biggest retailing companies in the world, can be classified as a mega-cap stock company. This type of stock (Large-cap and mega-cap stocks) tends to perform better in economic downturns. Still, when the economy materializes or pulls out from a recession, they are known to perform poorly when compared to small-cap stocks. Large-cap and mega-cap stocks appear to be less risky than mid-cap and small-cap stocks.

Small Vs. Mid Vs. Large-Cap Company – A Quick Comparison

We already know that Large-cap stocks have a $5 billion or more capitalization. They have the lowest risk when compared to other cap categorizations. This is because their resources can easily see them through any economic downturn. Mid-cap firms, on the other hand, have between $1bn and $5bn in capitalization. In the last few decades, mid-caps have outstripped both small and large-caps when it comes to stock performance, precisely because they are small during the growth process, which allows them to grow faster than the big-cap firms. Their size gives them breathing space so that in a period of recession, they are not as likely to go out of operation when compared to small-caps corporations. During the growth cycle, small-cap businesses have the edge over large-cap and mid-cap stocks. The stock price will grow along with the performance of the company. During and after the development phases, large-cap stocks may fall out of favor. Stock traders or Investors who pursue dividends regard them as dull and unadventurous.

The market cycle's peak period is a good time to shift the allocation from small-cap to big-cap. This is because the large-cap stocks are going to be relatively cheap. You will be able to hold onto them in the process of contraction. Although the price of all stocks may fall during every economic downturn, the small-caps stock may be forced to go out of business during this period. In essence, they don't have the resources to navigate through a prolonged period of low consumer spending.

During these economic downturns, they may even find it difficult to pay dividends that are accruing to shareholders. This is because all their assets are still required to grow. Hence, for investors who do not need regular income from their portfolio, small-cap companies may be a better shot than both mid and large-cap companies.

On the other hand, since small-cap firms are not as popular or well-known, so performing analysis may be quite strenuous for individual investors. Sadly, their past is smaller, and you may also have a tougher time identifying secondary media reports that a big-cap corporation would have. This is precisely why millions of investors go with a mutual fund for small-cap. Here, research and analysis are carried out by professionals who know the attributes which make a successful small-cap company. Investing in this way is considered better than doing this on your own.

Why Market Caps Matter

Stocks reflect ownership of corporations of varying sizes. When connecting the dots between the size of a company, the prospect of returns and threats is essential if you want to make a long-term investment plan. With this experience, you will be equipped to develop a balanced portfolio of stocks that contains a blend of market caps.

In general, market capitalization refers to the stage of overall business growth of a company, measuring their risk level and reward potential. Investments in large-cap stocks, for example, are generally considered more defensive than investment decisions made toward small-cap or mid-cap stocks, likely posing less risk in return for less rapid potential growth. Midcap stocks, in turn, generally fall on the risk/return spectrum between big-caps and small-caps. You may be asking why. As earlier stated, Midcap companies may be in the process of increasing market share and the improvement of their level of competitiveness. This period of growth is likely to decide if an organization will extend to its full capacity. Midcap stocks tend to fall in the risk/return range of large-caps and small-caps. Midcaps may offer more potential and more opportunities for growth than large-caps.

Relatively small assets of small-cap companies may make their stocks more vulnerable during an economic downturn and may also be susceptible to heavy competition and instability in untested markets. Regardless, small-cap stocks can offer substantial growth opportunities to long-term buyers, who can withstand short-term risky stock price movements. An easy way to accurately gauge an investment's success is to calculate its returns against those of an index that reflects identical investments. Indexes, just as with stocks, come in various sizes and forms. The Standard & Poor's (S&P) 500 is probably the most famous index for large-cap stocks. Like their names illustrate, the S&P Midcap 400 and S&P Small Cap 600 indexes reflect mid-cap and small-cap stocks, collectively. Another important benchmark for small-cap stocks is the Russell 2000.

Aside from determining the risky nature of an investment, market capitalization has also been applied by most investors to make the right investment combination. Over time, small-cap, midcap, and big-cap stocks have spent the past decade driving the market, more specifically because they can be affected by economic and financial trends in various ways. This is just precisely why most investors are diversifying their investments while keeping a mix of different market caps in their investment portfolios. If large-caps fall in value, small-caps or midcaps might be on their way up and might help offset any declines in the profits made.

No doubt, picking stock is an interesting game. However, it becomes risky if you don't diversify your investment with these market cap sizes. As a new stock trader or investor, you will be better off investing in a mix of stock caps.

To grow your network of portfolios using small-cap, midcap, and large-cap stocks, you may need to assess your financial objectives, risk profile, and some essential factors that are directly related to your investment decisions. A diverse portfolio that includes several market caps may help minimize risks in any given region and facilitate the achievement of your long-term financial objectives. Understanding how large, medium, and small businesses work together can help you make the right investment combinations. At the same time, going with an excellent long-term plan is the only way to get ahead in the stock market. Hence, maintaining a vital understanding of what's happening in your investments can enable you to make the best choices, and perhaps, assist you in handling any decisions made by your financial management agency. Note that this does not mitigate the risks of an investment or the risks of future losses of an investment.

Chapter Four: Stocks On The Move!

Momentum trading is a technique that employs the power of price changes as the foundation to open up positions in the market. However, while our primary focus in this book and chapter is on momentum trading, we must take some time to explore various trading strategies that are available to technical traders.

The truth is, mastering one trading style is quite essential, but, as a beginner, it is also necessary to have some fundamental knowledge of various trading types. This chapter outlines multiple trading types, with a significant focus on momentum trading.

Exploring Various Trading Types

There are several trading types that most technical investors seeking to profit from market volatility and changes may wish to use. The following outlines some brief descriptions of the most common trading types:

Long-Term Trading: Long-term trading is also known as position trading. It relates to the type of trading where investors may hold on to a given position for an extended period. This long-term trading can last from several weeks to a few years. The role of a long-term trader or investor is to determine if the existing pattern will continue for a much longer-term than momentum or price swing.

Long-term trading offers traders the luxury of time and freedom to trade: The opportunity for profit is not reduced, and long-term traders can make significant profits. These Position traders are not concerned with short-term volatility, because they assume their long-term investment horizons will smooth things out in the long run.

Position trading is the exact opposite of day trading, as the primary aim is to take advantage of the change in the dominant trend instead of the short-term movements that occur daily. However, while the method has proven effective for most pro-traders, this trading style might be a little complex for beginners.

Intraday Trading: Intraday or short-term trading entails buying and selling stocks on the same trading day. Stocks are bought here as well, but this time, not to invest in it, but to earn income by leveraging on the movement indices. Hence, variations in stock prices are used to make profits from the selling of securities. Day trading is often visualized as a fast and easy way to make money. Well, this is barely the case as intraday traders usually suffer extreme financial losses during their first months of trading. In severe cases, most intraday traders barely make a profit. This is simply because intraday traders are hampered by the distribution of bids, trading commissions as well as other expenses. These expenses can only allow them a few trading profits to break even.

Scalping: Scalping (or micro-trading) is a trading strategy that specializes in making minimal profits, continuously. This trading strategy seeks to make a significant amount of profit from small price volatility. It requires the trader to have some strict escape route because a massive loss can erase those several low earnings that the trader may have worked so hard to achieve. Anyway, for this strategy to be productive, it is essential to have the appropriate tools, like a direct-access broker, a live feed, and, of course, some amount of stamina for many trades. Scalping requires professional experience, and while many people find the idea appealing, I wouldn't recommend it for new traders who are still learning about stock trading.

Swing Trading: Swing trading is the art of identifying a pattern in the short term. It's a trading strategy that captures the returns on a given stock within a day and a week. Swing investors incorporate technical analysis into their search for stocks with short-term market momentum. In essence, they are barely interested in the basics or the inherent value of the stocks to be traded, but instead, they are much more interested in their price trends and patterns.

In summary, swing trading aims to capture a fraction of a future price movement or change. Whereas some investors are searching for volatile stocks with a series of movements or activities, other traders may prefer more placid stocks. In either case, swing trading involves finding where the asset's price is likely to move next, establishing a spot, and then obtaining a portion of the profit from such movement.

Momentum Trading: Momentum Investing is one of the most famous and conceptually clear forms of investment. In momentum trading, the trader detects a stock dropping and hops on to catch it, while capturing possible momentum as the stock makes its way up or down. Here, we concentrate on those stocks that are heading dramatically in one direction at considerable volume. The standard duration for this trading strategy is not specified in advance; we let the market and signals determine it, depending on how fast the stock moves and, of course, when the direction of the stock changes.

Our primary focus on this book is strictly on the momentum trading strategy. Hence we will be covering some fundamental concepts and strategies regarding this trading technique.

Momentum Trading – The Beginners Trading Muse!

Generally, the controversial word 'Momentum' is the rate or velocity of alterations in the price of a given stock, security, or tradable instrument. Momentum displays the level of change in price movements over a given period to help traders assess the intensity of the trend. However, stocks that tend to gravitate with momentum are commonly called momentum stocks.

In momentum trading, we take a long position in a stock or asset that has been trending upward. If the stock is trending downward, we take a short position

Momentum trading strategy is used by investors to trade uptrend stocks by going long (or buying stock) and short (or selling stock) downtrend. In other words, the stock may have a bullish momentum, which means that the price is going up, or bearish momentum, where the price is trending downward. Research has shown that momentum is much more effective in growing markets than in declining markets as stocks grow more often than they crash. In other words, every bull market appears to go on for a more extended period than the bear market.

Momentum is quite similar to a train, where the train speeds up gradually as it starts moving, but again slows down during the journey. Nonetheless, the train is moving, but at a higher velocity, as all the force built up from acceleration keeps driving it forward. Towards the end of the journey, the train eases up as it slows down.

In the stock market, most investors may get in to buy stock early, especially when the price is about to increase. Still, when the indicators come in, and it is evident to the investors that the stock has a growing potential, the price of this specific stock may increase tremendously. To momentum buyers, the most lucrative aspect of the trip is when prices move at high speed. Besides, after the sales and profits are recognized, the market generally changes its expectations. Thus, the price recurs or goes back to reflect the current financial performance of the organization.

In summary, momentum trading is a trading technique, whose holding time is only determined by the market and its signals. Thus, the holding time of each stock is hardly ever specified ahead of time. For example, we take a long position when the stock is trending upwards and a short position when the stock is trending downwards.

How Momentum Trading Strategy is Employed

There are several charting software packages and trading sites that can be used to evaluate the value of the stock so that traders do not have to estimate it often. Nevertheless, it is crucial to understand the parameters that go into these equations to fully understand what variables are used to evaluate the momentum or pattern of the stock.

In its simple expression, momentum can be measured using the formula below:

Momentum = $V - Vx$

Where V = latest stock price, Vx = closing price, and x = number of days ago

Momentums are measured across longer durations of weeks or months or shorter time frames. Using one of the multiple applicable momentum indicators, you can establish an access point for the purchase (or sale) of the equity you want to trade. You may also want to create a beneficial and rational exit point for this trade based on the estimated levels of market support and resistance. Also, it is recommended that stop-loss orders are placed over or beneath their point of entry — depending on the movement or changes of exchange. This will help guide against unexpected losses and price trend reversals.

Momentum Trading Indicators

The momentum indicators are standard tools that are employed to evaluate the momentum of a given stock. They are graphical instruments that can be used to demonstrate and predict how quickly the price of a specific security moves towards a direction, in addition to whether these price movements will continue along the same path.

The concept behind this device is that, as securities are exchanged in the exchange market, the pace of price movements is as high as possible when the introduction of new traders or capital into a given trade is approaching its maximum limit.

Momentum indicators can be used to determine the best time to invest in a given stock. The following are some technical tools that can help you get started with momentum trading.

- **The Relative Strength Index (RSI):** Just like the name suggests, it is used to analyze the resilience of current price movements over current periods. The ultimate goal is to demonstrate the probability that the current trend will be substantial compared to the previous performance.

- **Stochastic**: The stochastic oscillator evaluates the current value of the asset to its value over a given period. When the trend lines within these oscillators hit over-sold requirements— usually below twenty — it implies that an upward price movement is ahead. On the other hand, when they hit over-purchased requirements — usually reading over 80—it means that a declining price trend is ahead. In simple terms, this is known as the indicator line. It also makes use of the signal line, so that if the signal line and the indicator line cross each other, then a possible change in direction may occur.

▢ **Moving Averages**: These can be used to determine the general price patterns and momentum by straightening what may seem to be chaotic market moves on short-term charts into more readable visible trends. They are calculated by attaching the closing prices across a specific number of periods and separating the result by the number of periods considered.

▢ **Moving Average Convergence Divergence (MACD):** This method evaluates the fast-moving and slow-moving exponential market average trend lines on the chart against the signal axis. This shows all price momentum and its available price trend reversal positions. When these positions do not move further, momentum is perceived to be stable, but when they converge, momentum is reducing, and the price starts to move toward a reversal.

The points below are made for further learning and visual chart reading:

Why Momentum Trading Should Be Your Best Shot

Momentum trading will result in massive gains for an investor with the right experience, personality, and skill, more specifically, one who can deal with the risks involved when following a momentum trading strategy. The perks may include the following:

High-Profit Potential in a Limited Time: Suppose that the stock purchased rises from $35 to $47.50 due to an overly definite analyst article; you may sell this stock at a profit of 50 percent before the price itself is reversed.

Taking Advantage of Market Fluctuations: Momentum trading is about focusing on the momentum of market trends, searching for stocks that are about to rise, by buying and selling them before prices begin to fall.

Taking Advantage of Other Investor's Emotional Decisions: Rather than being guided by an emotional reaction like many traders, you can easily make good use of this emotional reaction, by making a profit on the changing prices of emotional traders.

Beginners Friendly: Generally, trading involves a high degree of risk that can make new investors lose a massive amount of money. Sadly, most new traders make numerous losses when trading stocks for the very first time.

However, the allure of momentum trading is the fact that beginners can earn massively working only 2-3 hours a day. Thus, for new and aspiring stock investors seeking financial freedom and independence, I recommend you adopt a specific investment strategy, and one of the easiest ways to go about this is through momentum trading.

It requires a high level of discipline to trade stocks using this trading strategy since traders must close a trade at the first weakness signal, while funds available are allocated to a trade indicating strength. However, when done correctly, momentum trading can generate mouth-watering returns to traders.

I will be exploring some essential strategies that can help you stay at the top of your game as a momentum trader.

Chapter Five: Institutions Can *'Make'* or *'Mar'* You

Institutional investors are a dominant force in the financial world. They dictate supply and demand in the marketplace and play a vital role in the pricing of financial assets, more specifically, stocks. It is, therefore, worthwhile learning about what motivates this dynamic group of actors, as well as how they play a significant role in affecting your investment decision. In this chapter, I will be exploring the essentials of institutional investors and their impact on the stock market.

Who are Institutional Investors?

Institutional investors are entities that pool funds on behalf of others and invest them in several different securities or groups of assets. They are a non-bank company, entity, or association that purchases and sells securities on behalf of its members. These market participants tend to invest in large quantities to qualify for special treatment, such as commissions and faster implementation rates. They provide massive benefits to investors and members who historically lacked the means to access a more significant global market. For this effect, institutional investors have a crucial role to play in how stocks operate and how these assets are valued.

Institutional Investors vs. Retail Investors

Stock trading can be as basic as hitting the purchase or sale button on a stock trading platform. Nonetheless, more advanced traders can choose more sophisticated transactions by fixing a price limit for a block trade that is analyzed over several brokers and exchanged across several days. As we already know, this can be done through a retail trader or an institutional investor.

Retail traders trade securities with a personal account. Of course, these are the likes of you and I. Institutional traders, on the other hand, trade on behalf of the company or institution accounts they manage. Pension funds, insurance firms, and mutual funds are some common examples of institutional investors.

While there are some underlying benefits of institutional traders over retail investors, the benefits enjoyed have depleted over time. The breach between these two has been reduced by the proliferation of advanced electronic brokerages, the ability to exchange and obtain more complex securities (like options), updated information, and the global availability of financial data and analysis. Well, the breach between these two has not closed completely. Institutional investors have some level of advantages over retail traders, and to some extent, they play a significant role in the market as well. The capacity to influence trading fees, the ability to provide members with the best trading

85

prices, and overall performance of trading sessions are all essential benefits of institutional traders. They evaluate essential point charges for every exchange that should be made and allow only an optimum price and implementation for each session. Marketing or delivery cost rates are not charged either.

Due to the enormous volume of funds that are pooled periodically, institutional investors can have a significant impact on the security share price. For this purpose, trades may sometimes be shared between different traders to avoid having a material effect on the market.

The bigger the mutual fund, the larger the market capitalization most institutional traders may hold. It is harder to put a vast amount of funds to work in small-cap stocks since it may be difficult to own a majority of the shares or reduce the value to the position where no one is willing to buy the stock offered for sales in the exchange.

On the other hand, retail traders usually trade stocks, shares, futures, and options; at the same time, they may equally have little or no entry to IPOs. For institutional traders, most of the transactions are carried out within lot sizes (e.g., 100 shares), but retailers can exchange any number of stocks at one time.

The operating cost of doing business is typically higher for retailers since they are required to trade via the help of a stockbroker who generally charges marketing and distribution fees, and a given fee per trade. The amount of stock exchanged by retailers is usually too small to have an impact on the security price.

Retail investors can easily buy into a small-cap corporation since these companies are generally known to have smaller price positions that enable them to acquire a range of securities that allow a balanced and diversified portfolio.

Types of Institutional Investors

The majority of market observers recognize six varieties of institutional investors. A brief overview of each of them is provided below.

- **Pensions:** Pension funds are one of the significant institutional asset owners, with over $40 trillion in assets under their management as of 2018. Here, funds are divided along various lines, including state, corporate, public, and union. Pension funds receive payments from investors and sponsors, whether public or private and promise to disburse a retirement benefit to the beneficiaries of the fund at an agreed period in the future.

- **Insurance Companies**: Insurance firms are also another institutional investor that utilizes the benefits paid to their customers to maximize their profits. These organizations, which include casualty insurers and life insurance companies, receive premiums from clients to shield policyholders against different types of unforeseen hazards. They spend the premiums generated on relevant tasks while providing a basis for potential claims and benefits.

- **Endowment Funds**: Schools, foundations, and other non-profit institutions are also known as institutional investors. Such organizations are financed by subscriptions, grants, and charitable donations for a specific cause or purpose. Endowments are structured in such a way that the principal balance remains unchanged. However, investment income or a small part of the principal is available for use on an annual basis.

- **Commercial Banks**: Financial institutions such as JP Morgan Chase & Co. and Bank of America also fall under this category of institutional investors. They control more than $1 trillion in assets.

These institutions take deposits from their depositors and then make loans available to others who are willing to pay a certain amount of interest. Some of these loans may include mortgages, lines of credit, or business loans.

- **Mutual Funds**: A mutual fund is an open-ended investment firm that gathers funds from individual investors into a single fund managed by a portfolio manager. These pooled investments are often used to buy a range of investment products, including stocks, bonds, and currencies. They are a high-risk investment when compared to mutual funds and are tentative to various types of government regulations

- **Hedge Funds**: Hedge funds are categorized as institutional investors and alternative investments, where pooled capital is employed to access above-market returns. Hedge funds are typically different from mutual funds. They are known to be alternative investments because regulators do not restrict their usage of shares purchased. While these may have some close similarities to private equity funds, it is important to note that they vary significantly, since a vast amount of hedge funds are pulled into fairly liquid investment. Nevertheless, funds that function in the same way as hedge funds but are governed in the same way as mutual funds are available and are regarded as liquid alternative investments.

Institutional investors have a tremendous impact on stock prices as they account for most of the trading; their purchases can increase a stock price, while their stock sales can send a stock price down. Institutional talk can also influence stock prices, though its effect may only have a short-term impact on retail investors. Let's take some time to explore their impact on stock performance.

Stock Purchases: Institutional buying leaves some level of impact on stock prices. In other words, their stock purchases are what propel stock prices. Once a stock is popular with companies, they begin to build positions therein. The higher the value of a stock increases, the more institutions are forced to have it in their portfolios.

Security Sales: Conversely, if a given stock did not act as expected — probably by reporting results that are below investors' expectations or they reveal some awful news— institutional selling can lead to a considerable drop in the price of a stock. Sometimes these investors can plan their purchases for weeks or even months, leading to a consistent but yet, gradual rise in stock price; they often all want to go out at once and generate a stampede for sales. Stock will take months to advance 20 or 30 percent on institutional purchasing and lose that much on institutional sales in just a day or two.

Stock Price Support: Since their purchases can increase the price of a stock, institutions avoid overpaying for the stocks they buy by spacing their purchases over a given period, say days or weeks, while squeezing up all available stock at the prices they like. Sometimes they buy "on dips," when a stock is undergoing a slight decline. Their purchasing puts a floor beneath the price of a stock, restricting its downslide. If an institution has a significant stock position, it can also act as a support system to the stock price, by buying more shares to prevent the stock from declining.

Window Dressing: The institutions announce quarterly results. Their assets are included in a report which goes out to the investors at the end of every quarter. To appear perfect, institutions are buying stocks that have increased over time and selling those that are declining, a practice that is commonly referred to as "window dressing." Window dressing will trigger short-term fluctuations in the last days of a quarter, which may create buying and selling opportunities for smart investors.

Talking Stock Prices Up or Down: Institutional discourse or predictions can also influence stock prices over the short term. A favorable mention in a TV interview by a money manager or an upgrade by an analyst will send a stock price up, whereas a downgrade by an analyst will send down a stock price. When acting on institutional projections or discourse, you should be cautious, because it is likely to benefit them on both a long and short term basis and not you. An institution can decide to talk up a stock that has a high position to accelerate the price and generate additional demand so it can sell. On the other hand, a reduction may be designed to send a stock price down so that the institution can purchase these stocks at a cheaper rate.

Institutional investors have a great impact on stock and other investment instruments since individuals looking to make suitable gains from the market place premiums on technical experts.

This does not mean that individual or retail traders are not making significant gains from the market. If you can follow the strategies outlined in this book, you are sure to earn those *watering* returns. Either way, checking for institutional sponsorship on an investment can keep you abreast of those stocks with an increased demand. You can visit investors.com to check for institutional sponsorships on a stock or an asset.

Part Two

High-Performance Stocks

Chapter Six: Unraveling the Price and Value Puzzle

High-performance stocks are essential to every momentum traders. And by high-performance stocks, I mean those companies with quarterly and annual earnings growth, the highest return on equity, the most extensive profit margins, and the most substantial sales growth. However, to assess the value of a stock as well as when to go in or out of the market, various methods can be used to achieve this assessment. And a major way to go about it is through fundamental analysis.

By analyzing the associated financial and economic variables, traders look at the intrinsic value of the stock via the help of fundamental analysis (FA). Analysts then check other factors that may alter the value of the stock. For instance, they can decide to study the macroeconomic elements such as the economic impact on the industry or microeconomic factors such as the sales performance of an organization yearly.

The good thing is that we will be exploring everything on fundamental analysis, and explain how you can start using it for your momentum trading sections. But before we go any further, we must examine the fundamental relationships between the price and value of a stock.

The Price vs. Value

Stock market participants' infrequent cases try to resolve the gap between the value of a given stock and its price. If you have spent any time deeply immersed in stock market news and trends, you will realize that value and price are two commonly used measures in the stock market.

You remember the popular saying: "Don't judge a book by its cover?" Well, there are some equally valid words of wisdom which can be applicable for any momentum trader or investor: in the same way, you shouldn't judge a stock by its price. With the vast amount of information available to investors, many people often incorrectly assume that a stock with a small-dollar price is cheap. In contrast, another with a more substantial price is costly. This notion has succeeded massively in leading both new and existing investors down the wrong path. Not to worry, we will be exploring some essentials that relate to the price and value of a stock and explain how you can also make reasonable investment decisions using the information at your disposal.

Other Drivers of Stock Prices

While various factors can influence market prices, the following are just some that should be taken note of:

- The expectations of market participants' expectations which may include the overall market trends,

- Analyst estimates,

- News,

- good or bad economy,

- ☐ Monetary policy,

- ☐ Confidence or lack of confidence in the marketplace,

- ☐ Company news, such as earnings, financial issues, or scandals.

For ease of understanding, I have decided to explain the most common drivers of stock prices in the following point below:

Economic News and Reports: Other forces can affect the price of a stock, and induce immediate or temporary price changes. Some of these forces may affect corporate events and market reports. While some market reports may have a positive and negative report on stock prices, not all market reports or economic news can act on the price of a stock.

Behavioral Instinct: the price of a stock can also be fueled by what called behavioral instinct. It is defined as a common inclination for risk aversion traders to imitate the trading activity of a larger group. For example, if a large proportion of a given group decides to sell a stock, and it reduces the prices, other traders may decide to perform a similar action, believing that these large investors are correct about their market predictions. The reverse occurs when a large group decides to buy a given stock. In a situation of behavioral instinct, there may be no form of technical or fundamental analysis for price increases. However, investors are still selling because everyone is doing so, and they may become obviously terrified of losing out.

In most cases, the price of a given stock is usually consistent with analysts' projected value. Still, it is also important to note that every piece of news or economic change can only result in quick price changes in the short term.

Exploring the Value of a Stock

As far as stocks are concerned, market traders may assess the value of the stock by studying variables like

- The earnings projection of a company,

- The company market dominance,

- Its sales report over a specific period,

- Potential and existing rivals,

- Measurements like the P/E ratio

- Analysis of publications by analysts who track the company.

Quite a number of these analyses follow a straightforward and simplistic approach (see chapter eight). Stock market traders earn excellent salaries, carrying out research, including the potential for ups and downs in the stock market. During this process, a trader can reach a value, which is what they believe should be the optimum value of a stock.

Value on Price

In frequent cases, the actual price of the stock is projected within the trader's estimated value, except short term fluctuations attributable to an upward or declining market.

However, there are several occasions when the price of the stock exchanged on the open market varies significantly from its real value. The trading price of the stock is the amount that a prepared seller and buyer find acceptable to each faction. Simply put, the real value of a stock is defined by the price a trader is ready to pay.

The Efficient Market Hypothesis (EMH) is the backbone of a substantial part of today's financial theory. According to this principle, the price of each commodity on the financial markets represents all the information provided and trades at its fair value.

According to this principle, it is not possible to find stocks that are overvalued or undervalued. This is because the price of a given stock equals its value when the market is active. If this principle were valid, no one would be able to make excess returns or beat the market. The real-world market situation, however, shows a different image, since a lot of investors repeatedly beat the market with little or no difficulties.

Why the Difference between Stock Prices and Value?

While it is quite easy to believe that the value of the stock relies extensively on the price of the stock, it is also important to note that there is a fine line between the two, specifically in the short term. However, the critical distinction between price and value is that the price is subjective, while the value of a stock is fundamental. The price of a stock relies on the market, which changes daily and does not accurately reflect the value of the company. On the other hand, the value of a stock, which is the actual value of the product, is calculated by an in-depth analysis of the company's business, including fundamental analysis and the analysis of future predictions.

Getting a precise figure for the stock value is not an easy process, and in fact, may require a challenging process. Seeing that it is quite complicated and essentially meaningless, there is rarely a view on how much of a given stock should be put up for sale or bought at a particular point in time. This means that the market is often volatile, and in this case, the stock value and the stock price are not the same.

Generally, momentum traders depend largely on price movements, regardless of the market directions. In other words, they earn substantial profit by taking advantage of the direction of a stock price. They make a massive profit by finding out how these changes in price can occur over time. However, other Investors like value investors are much more concerned about value as their value calculation can direct their decisions when trading any stock over the long term. This does not mean buying and forgetting, as the market evolves at a fast pace. While our primary focus is on momentum trading, both traders and investors must reassess the value of their shares regularly.

Taking this procedure will make it difficult if you decide to hold or buy a plummeting stock or make the error of selling a stock with high potential. We will be explaining more about how you can assess the value and price of a stock, to make the best out of your trading sessions.

Chapter Seven: Picking Great Companies for Stock Investing

Exploring the Basics

Fundamental analysis involves studying a company's integral or essential financial level, more specifically, organizational revenue, profits, growth potential, assets, debt, management, goods, and competition. This type of analysis explores a business' leading indicators to assess its financial health, which gives you an idea of its stock's worth.

To evaluate these stocks for investment purposes, many investors use fundamental analysis alone or in conjunction with other instruments. The goal is to assess the present value, and more significantly, how the market prices the stock. Generally, the fundamental analysis takes into account only those factors that are directly connected to the business itself, rather than the general market condition or the details of the technical analysis.

Still, here I will present a top-down approach to the usual fundamental analysis.

This will generally involve analyzing the general economic condition as a whole and then moves down to specific businesses from industry groups. It is worth noting that all knowledge is subjective as part of the research process. Certain industry groups and firms are compared to other businesses. It is also essential to compare organizations in the same category as others.

More importantly, an overall assessment of the general economy will be done in a top-down approach. However, most industry groups and companies benefit and grow as the economy expands. An investor should narrow these findings down to those groups that are best suited to benefit from the present or future economic environment. If most businesses are predicted to benefit from an increase, then equity risk will be relatively low, and a growth-oriented aggressive strategy might be desirable. These growth strategies may involve buying technology, biotech, semiconductor, and cyclical stocks.

If the market is projected to contract, an investor can opt for a more conservative approach and look for stable revenue-oriented firms. A defensive strategy may involve buying consumer staples, utilities, and energy-related inventories. To evaluate the potential of an industry group, an investor may have to consider the overall rate of growth, market size, and economic importance. Although the individual company is still relevant, its industry group will likely have just as much or more impact on the stock price.

Ideally, as stocks move, they move in groups. Once the industry group is chosen, an investor will need to narrow down the company list before moving to a much more comprehensive analysis. Investors typically want to identify the leaders and innovators within a given stock group.

The first step is to recognize the existing business, the future trends within the organization, and its competitiveness. How well does the organization rank according to market dominance, product status, and the competitive edge over other businesses? Get to know the current leader and how the decisions made affect the current balance of power within the sector. What are the Entry Barriers? Success depends on each edge, whether it's marketing, technology, market dominance, or innovation. A competitive competition study within a market can help to determine those firms that have an advantage, and those that are most likely to maintain their lead. At this point, you will have a shortlist of companies, and the final step in this analysis process would be to break down the financial statements and come up with a means of valuation. Some of these popular ratios are to be estimated by splitting the stock price via a unique value driver.

Fundamental Analysis Tools and Factors

Many people think that fundamental analysis in stock trading is a common number concept, like a company's revenue. However, fundamental analysis can include everything from company management quality to other factors, like its market share and dominance.

For easy understanding, I will be classifying these varieties of fundamental factors into quantitative and qualitative factors. The contextual meanings of these factors are not far from the usual basic understanding you are familiar with.

Qualitative fundamental factors: They are those fundamental factors that are based on quality and cannot be measured in numerical terms. I will be reviewing three major fundamental factors that you should look out for when choosing great companies for your stock investment game. These factors include:

▢ **Competitive Advantage:** A business ability to continuously succeed is largely dependent on its ability to sustain its competitive advantage over other related businesses. A company may have a competitive advantage over other businesses if it can offer a unique product and service at a low cost. If a company has a competitive advantage over relative businesses in the same industry, they can grow and maintain their income. At the same time, stock investors or shareholders are properly rewarded through stable or increased investment returns over time.

▢ **Management:** To most stock traders and investors, a company management capacity is a major criterion when investing in a company. Truly, an organization's business model can barely thrive if a company business model is not properly executed with the help of top management professionals. A business is nothing without experienced management or top executives. It may be difficult to assess the professional expertise of these top executives as a retail or individual investor. However, an easy way to assess this is through the organization's website, which will allow you to assess the resumes of top executives and board members. More so, the past job performed by these top executives has a lot to say about their level of management, professionalism, and expertise.

🔲 **Corporate Governance/Policies**: The corporate policies of an organization specify the relationships and responsibilities that exist between top management of an organization, directors, and its stakeholders. Of course, no trader or investor will want to buy into a firm without a proper work ethic and transparency. Ensure the communications between the organization top executives and management are clearly stated and transparent.

Quantitative Fundamental factors: As the name implies, fundamental quantitative factors are usually expressed in numerical terms. They are measurable characteristics of a business that depict the company's performance in terms of sales, profits, and earnings. Simply put, they are those numerical factors that measure the financial performance of a company. The most commonly used financial statements, in this case, are cash flow statements, income statements, and balance sheets. I will explain them briefly in the points below.

1. **Cash flow statement:** The cash flow statement is considered the most important quantitative factor of a company as it shows the cash inflow and outflow of a company over a given period. While a company's accountant can easily maneuver their earnings, it is difficult to manipulate the figures displayed in a company bank

account statement. A cash flow statement focuses on the following activities in a business:

- **Cash from financing**: Cash inflow or outflow received or paid from borrowing or lending funds.

- **Operating cash flow:** Cash inflow and outflow generated from the daily operational activities of a business.

- **Cash from investing**: It includes both proceeds generated and cash used in the sales of business assets and long-term equipment.

2. **The balance sheet:** A company's balance sheet depicts the available assets, liability, and equity. Assets are the resources owned by the business at a given period, including machinery, cash, buildings, and inventory. On the other hand, liabilities are debt owed by the company, while equities are the total amount contributed by owners.

3. **Income statement:** Unlike the balance sheet, the income statement provides an in-depth analysis of a company's performance over a given period. The income statement provides detailed information on business income, expenditures, and profit generated as a result of the daily activities over a specific period.

Thus, these quantitative factors depict the business sales profits and earnings over a given period.

Common Tools for Fundamental Analysis

While earnings are a major determinant for stock growth, they don't tell you a lot on their own. Earnings do not pinpoint how the market values the stock.

When buying stock, you're going to need more fundamental analysis tools to build a snapshot of how an individual stock is valued.

You can find that most of these ratios have already been completed for you on finance-related websites, but still, they are really not difficult to determine on your own. Keep in mind that the most commonly used tools of fundamental analysis emphasize on earnings, growth, and market value. Here, we will be discussing the most widely used fundamental analysis tools that can be used to determine the value of the stock during each trade.

Earnings per Share (EPS)

In a recent study on high-performing stocks, 75% of corporations used in this study recorded an increase in their earnings. However, after a few years, these stocks showed a quick fall in their market performance, which led to a fall in their value. The truth is that an organization's earnings alone are not sufficient enough when determining the value of high performing stocks. Even profit gains of 5% to 10% are insufficient to fuel a significant price movement in a stock. A company showing an increase of as little as 8% or 10% is more likely to report lower or slower earnings suddenly in the next quarter.

- ⬜ Here is a quick tip - You shouldn't be concerned with the company's total net income, because you don't own the whole organization anyway. So, avoid falling for an organization's report and profit increment. What matters is the current quarter earnings per share compared to the same quarter the year before.

Among other fundamental analysis tools, earning per share is one of the most commonly used tools by most investors and stock market players. This measure is equally important to income-focused investors seeking a steady source of income. The term provides a clear view of the value of a company's stock. It is defined as the portion of the profit that is allocated to each company's share. This is calculated by dividing the total profit accruing to a firm by the number of outstanding shares in a company.

Earnings can trigger an increase in the price of a stock, and investors, on the other hand, can make money when these prices increase. Hence, if a company has high earnings per share, it means that it has more money available either for reinvestment in the business or distribution to shareholders in the form of dividend payments. In either case, investors will win. In its simple terms, when the earnings per share of a company are increasing or high, it simply means that the profitability of the company is expanding.

Earnings per share can be calculated in two ways. They are either calculated by dividing the net income tax by the total number of outstanding shares or by subtracting the net income after tax from total dividends and divided by the total number of outstanding shares, this is known as the weighted EPS. I recommend using the weighted EPS when calculating the earning per share ratio. This is because a company's outstanding share changes over time. To get an idea of the best performing share within the same industry, you should compare various companies within the same industry when using an EPS. This will give you an idea of the best-performing stocks within the same industry. For example, the EPS Score of 99 means that the company has outperformed 99 percent of all other companies in terms of annual and recent quarterly earnings results.

No doubt, when the earnings per share of a company are increasing, it means that the company's financial status is a good one and may worth the effort of an investor. Just like every other measure for determining the financial status of a corporation, the ratio has its shortcomings. For example, since an organization can buy back their shares, they can work on their EPS by bringing down the number of outstanding shares without necessarily expanding their income level. For this reason, businesses can mislead investors to believe that their financial status is a good one. Also, EPS does not take into account considerations such as the outstanding debt of a company.

More than this, the onetime extraordinary gain is barely captured in this report, for example, the sale of a company's real estate. EPS does not take into account the fund required for generating the earnings under consideration. For instance, if two corporations depict equal EPS value, but one of these two utilizes lower capital to generate the same income, the corporation with lower capital is likely to manage its assets better than its equivalent. However, this simple analogy cannot be mirrored in its EPS value.

However, while this is an important fundamental analysis tool, it is best when used with other analytical tools.

Return on Equity

"Green Mountain Coffee Roasters" alone generated a profit of more than 113 percent this year. But in cases where powerful momentum stocks are increasing upwards, it may not be very easy to know when to get on board. But it's not as complicated as you are often made to believe.

If you want the inside track of the best momentum stocks with ultra-explosive gains, throw your "lenses" out and concentrate on one of the most useful financial ratios in the world of stock investing.

It's called return on equity (ROE); the term simply throws more light in the world of investment.

ROE is one of the best metrics commonly used by most investors and momentum traders to measure the productivity of a company. This tells you how much income the organization makes from the capital the shareholders have invested. Well, let me show you how easy it is to pull this number out – and how lucrative this essential metrics can be to most momentum traders. You can measure the return on equity (ROE) of a given stock by dividing the net income of a company by the equity of its shareholders. The higher the amount derived, the more successful the company is in turning its assets and workers into wads of cash for investors.

For example, Dell Computer's highly efficient direct sales and high-profit margin approach paid off between 1998 and 2003 in terms of strong earnings growth and a double-digit ROE of 46%. At the same time, Dell's shares increased 91.95 percent by raining capital on shareholders. ROE explains why the company - Green Mountain Coffee Roasters (NASDAQ: GMCR) had a return of over 92 percent while the S&P500 had a profit of-34.37 percent over the last year. It's been a rough period for most investors, but GMCR shareholders had a lot to smile about as management skillfully squeezed out over 27 percent return on equity. Green Mountain is one of the few safe places for any investors to ride out the market's storm of the century.

Mathematically, Equity Return can be expressed as Net Income or Profit /Shareholder's Equity.

Nevertheless, the only way such a measure can remain high or improve with time is to sustain or increase the bottom line net profit via proper organizational management and structure. When executives want to hose creditors by pulling some income away–selling more shares through a seasoned stock sale–you can easily capture them by a decline in this ratio. On the other hand, other investors who focus exclusively on net income will not know that the end is near because the net income of the company will remain the same over time, regardless of the changes in the ROE ratio. This is just exactly why this ratio is a better indicator of management efficacy in bringing the cheese home.

Return on Equity (ROE) is quite easy to track through several financial platforms. From my end, I make use of Yahoo! Finance and other financial platforms, which I have been exploring in other chapters as we have progressed. However, for illustration's sake, I will be using Yahoo! Finance. In the first step, you may have to type the stock symbol of the company you are searching for in the "Get Quotas" section on the top left of the web page.

When you see the corporation's information section, click the "Key Statistics" reference. Also, on the same page in the "Management Effectiveness" column, you will see the importance of the "Return on Equity (ttm)" segment, which shows you how well management produces income for shareholders.

In summary, a higher return on equity (ROE) figure shows us how well management is performing as well as detecting if a company is undervalued. Hence you must observe how ROE changes over time; you really want to see it increase. Download and save the Yahoo! Finance Web page for "Main Statistics" every week, and you'll see for yourself how the return on equity shifts. If the return on equity depicts a double-digit and also increasing, you might want to consider buying the stock.

Cash Flow Ratio

Most investors believe that the cash flow ratios are a better measure of value than some other fundamental analysis ratio as an essential measure of the market. This is because it serves as an easy way to detect an organization's ability to pay dividends.

Generally, cash flow can be defined as the net income of the business - the difference between sales and purchases during a given period - plus depreciation (an accounting technique that disperses the cost of a fixed asset across several years) while adding the value of many other non-cash assets like intangible assets, including copyright patents, trademarks, etc.

Companies, like every other entity, need cash to survive. And, of course, they need money to pay dividends.

But they also need money to pay for all the resources that have been used in the past and present for the proper functioning of the business as well as making capital improvements while paying operational expenses like wages, raw materials or fuel for company cars, etc.

Organizations with a high level of debt are required to pay a large amount of interest to service their debt. If an opportunity unexpectedly occurs, perhaps to purchase a densely populated piece of land or a business that would help the company in some way, cash-poor companies may not have the funds to make the offer. More importantly, perhaps, the companies with a cash reserve and continuous inflow are more likely to thrive in "difficult periods." Companies that have the cash to do whatever they want are in a better position to make sound business decisions, keep their business afloat, and emerge in a tougher difficult market.

When you begin to draw up an image on what you want in the stock, the information obtained from a fundamental analysis can be used as performance metrics to measure the value of potential investments. Since the most commonly used fundamental report focuses on an organization's earnings, growth, and market value, consider the market assessment of the entire industry and the general market situations instead of just the individual stock market. The success of a given business is strongly affected by the sector and the prevailing market conditions.

Chapter Eight: Identifying Stock Market Turning Points with Value Strategies

If you want to enjoy mouth-watering ROI (returns on investment) as a momentum stock trader, you may need to grasp a few useful tips and be prepared to do some extra digging during your free time. One of the essential skills you may need to learn is how to determine the market value of a stock. In the absence of this skill, stock traders are left to dance in the winds of the market without a strong basis, not knowing whether a company's growth predictions are fixed on the stock quote or whether the stock of a company is undervalued. This idea of losing millions in investment is what scares the hell out of me.

Ideally, virtually every article in the business news can be categorized as redundant framework chaos. Still, truth be told, an investor should have a working procedure to determine the real value of the stock. For this reason, we must take a closer look at some resources that most momentum traders and investors have traditionally used to determine the value of company stock and how you can start using them in evaluating both valued and undervalued stocks.

Why You Should Determine the Value of Stocks before Buying

When purchasing such fractional holdings from a given business, it is crucial to note that the underlying value of the stock is not linked directly to its market price. However, most investors and analysts will make you believe they are. In reality, a lot of investors endorse the theory of an efficient market, the theory that asserts that every studied fact is currently priced in the value of the stock. The consequence of this principle is that winning the market can be likened to a flip of the coin and not a case of professional stock collection.

Most of the supporters of this hypothesis propose buying into an ETF or an index fund due to the current near-impossible task of having the odds in your favor. It is impossible to question such a principle.

Passive investment in an index fund allows market participants to diversify into several stocks easily, providing access to the stock market's historical returns.

But, it doesn't take long to detect the flaws in this concept.

For example, how does the so-called theory take recent stock market crashes and fluctuations into account? Years back, the Dow Jones Industrial Average plummeted by more than 500 points in just a single trading session, which led to a decrease in its value after a few years. So here is the question, if this theory was valid, why would it be so difficult to account for the rapid decrease in a single trading session? Well, unless the stock was highly undervalued after the fall or massively overvalued before the collapse.

Alternatively, active investors claim that the market moves on a routine basis towards elation and dysphoria. Benjamin Graham, the founder of a popular investment principle called value investment, stressed this dimension of the stock market, claiming it consistently undervalued and overvalued the stocks of listed companies. Investment gurus believe that the price of a given stock differs significantly from its value. To define the value and price of each stock, they employ a series of metrics. We will be exploring more on this, but before I go any further, I will take a moment to explore the basics of stock market value.

The Concept of Market Value

Market value commonly regarded as OMV or "open market valuation" is the price that an asset would have gained on the exchange or the value that the investment community gives to a specific stock or company. The Market value for exchange-traded instruments like stocks is quite easy to calculate because their exchange rates or market prices of these stocks are widely distributed and readily available. Still, for some 'off the counter instruments' like fixed income securities, they are usually challenging to determine.

The market value of a company is a clear indicator of the investor's view of its financial prospects. The variety of market values on the market is massive, running the gamut from less than $1 million for the smallest companies to hundreds of billions for the largest and most influential companies around the globe.

Market value can vary considerably over different periods and is significantly affected by the market cycle. Market values decline in bear markets that involve economic downturns, and on the other hand, the market value increases in bull markets that occur during economic expansions. Market value also depends on several specific factors, such as the industry where the company operates, its performance, debt burden, and the broad market setting.

For instance, Company Y and Company Z may have $100 million in annual revenue, but if Y is a quickly and smoothly-growing technology company and Z is a hidebound supermarket; no doubt, Company Y market value would be considerably higher than that of Company Z (attributable to its technical input).

In the illustration above, Company Z may trade multiple sales of 5, which would give a market value of $500 million. At the same time, Company Y may trade multiple sales of 2, which would also give it a market value of $200 million.

The market value of a firm may differ substantially from its book value. A stock may probably be considered undervalued if its market value is far below its book value, which also indicates that the stock is exchanged at a deep discount on the book value per share. On the other hand, this does not suggest that the stock is overvalued if it is exchanged or traded at a book value premium, as this relies on the sector and the severity of the premium with the peers of the stock.

Market value can be determined by valuation techniques or multiples provided by investors to businesses; some of them include price-to-earnings, price-to-sales, Enterprise value-to-EBITDA, and so on. We will be exploring some of them in the section below.

Price to Earnings Ratio

The price-to-earnings ratio (P/E ratio) is one of the most commonly used ratios for the valuation of a stock, which measures its current share price relative to its earnings per share (EPS). The price-to-earnings ratio is often referred to as multiple prices or multiple earnings. It can also be used to equate business with its historical record or to evaluate aggregate markets with one another or over a given period. Momentum traders and investors analyze the P/E ratio of the company when deciding whether the share price accurately represents the estimated earnings per share. The formula used for this analysis can be depicted below:

Price to Earnings Ratio (P/E) = Market Value Per Share/Earnings Per Share

To evaluate the P/E value, all you need to do is to split the current price of the stock (P) by its earnings per share (EPS) value. The value of the current stock price (P) can be derived by connecting the ticker sign of the stock of your choice into any finance website. Although this specific value represents what buyers have to pay for the stock, the EPS value is, to an extent, a more vaguely defined number.

EPS is used in two major variants. The topmost variant is a statistic in the fundamentals segment of virtually all finance websites; they often come with the expression "P/E (TTM)" where the expression "ttm" is a common stock market wordplay for "trailing twelve months." This value indicates a corporation's achievements in the past period (12 months). The other variant of EPS is included in the company's earnings report, which often sets limits and guidance to EPS. This variant is the corporation's informed estimate of what it hopes to make in the future.

Analysts also take an interest in long-term valuation patterns and find the metrics P/E 10 or P/E 30, which are measured over the last 10 or 30 years of earnings. Such metrics are commonly used to evaluate the total value of the stock index, such as the S&P 500 since these longer-term indicators will account for shifts in the business cycle. The P/E ratio of the S&P 500 plummeted around 6x (in 1949) to over 120x (in 2009.

Ironically, there is no P/E ratio clearly defined that renders a given stock a buy if it is below or a sale if it is above. Value investors and momentum traders will often consider several factors in the P/E ratio when making conclusions. For investors, the larger the gap between the intrinsic value of the stock and its current price, the higher the likelihood that the investor will regard the stock as a valuable venture. This is commonly known as the safety margin. More than this, the lower the value of the P/E ratio, the better. On the contrary, other investors like the growth investors or momentum trader are barely interested in buying into stock with low P/E ratios since stocks with these types of figures and the increased growth rates they hope for are unlikely to be found. These investors are more willing to purchase stocks with increasing P/E ratios, assuming that higher costs more than justify higher earnings growth.

Price to Sales Ratio

Traders often look for effective procedures to evaluate the value these given stocks to another, and another easy way to go about this is through the price to sales ratio. The price-to-sales (P/S) ratio uses the market capitalization and income of the company to establish if a given stock is valued correctly. The price-to-sales ratio is defined as the market price of the shares divided by the revenue generated by the sales of the products or services rendered by the company per share. A lot of investors prefer this metric to other means of measuring the market value of a stock. This is prone to the fact that sales figures of a company are a bit difficult to influence when compared to the earnings of a stock or the book value of the stock. In other words, the price-to-sales ratio is a more reliable measure of how the company operates. However, when the value of the EPS is negative or temporarily declining, the price-to-sale ratio is quite practical in this case, when compared to the P/E ratio. In this case, a low P/S may depict increasing earnings potential if the stock recuperates. The price-to-sales ratio can be utilized in predicting turnaround conditions or double-checking that the company's performance has not been overvalued. It is useful when a company starts to incur losses, and because of this, they barely have earnings that can be used by traders to evaluate their stock. According to most investment analysts, they are regarded as the 'king of value factors' and because of this, they work with a price to sales ratio that is remarkably lower than 1. This ratio is determined based on the Trailing Twelve Months (TTM).

While numerous benefits are accruing to this tool, this tool was misapplied over the last few years to support businesses with no revenue or profits. While earnings are often not a good indicator of an organization's financial viability, price to sales ratio may also be unreliable.

Comparing an organization's revenues on an apple-to-apple basis rarely works. However, to get the best out of what you want, the evaluation of sales must be paired with a meticulous examination of the company profit margins and a comparison of results with other firms in the same sector.

The EV/EBITDA Ratio

EBITDA is a short acronym for earnings before interest, taxes, depreciation, and amortization. The EBITDA is estimated before any other variables. In other words, interest and taxes are considered first. It doesn't include some variables like depreciation and amortization that are non-cash costs. Hence, the metric can give a clearer view of the financial performance of a business.

In some cases, it is used as a substitute to net income when determining the profitability of a product. The other aspect of the EV/EBITDA ratio is the Enterprise value. This is defined as the amount of equity or market capitalization of a company plus its debt minus cash.

EV is typically used to evaluate a company for a potential purchase or takeover, and the coefficient is computed by finding the ratio between EV and EBITDA; this is used to achieve a multiple cash flow ratio with more detail than the P/E ratio. This statistic is commonly used as a valuation technique; it measures the value of the business, along with its debt and liabilities, to its actual cash earnings. Higher ratio figures suggest that the business is undervalued.

Productive stock analysts barely look at just one statistic to assess the market value of a business, as well as to determine if a business is a worthwhile investment or not. As we have seen with the EV/EBITDA, the price to sales ratio, and P/E ratios, there are pros and cons for each metric. The values produced by these ratios can only reflect little without some interpretation and reflection on various factors that can affect the profitability and future outcomes of a corporation. To get the best result from these, they should be combined with other metrics to provide you with a good starting point and some useful insights as part of comprehensive stock analysis.

A Short message from the Author:

Hey, are you enjoying the book? I'd love to hear your thoughts!

Many readers do not know how hard reviews are to come by, and how much they help an author.

I would be incredibly grateful if you could take just 60 seconds to write a brief review on Amazon, even if it's just a few sentences!

>> Scan the Barcode with your phone camera to leave a quick review;

Thank you for taking the time to share your thoughts!

Your review will genuinely make a difference for me and help gain exposure for my work.

Chapter Nine: Predicting Market Swings With Technical Analysis

How about I told you that you could predict the market and make mouth-watering profits on an investment?

According to most traders and investors, the best and straightforward approach to momentum trading is through technical analysis, especially when you want to look at investment and identify opportunities. This grossly examines statistical trends focused on trading activities. For instance, they may evaluate historical oscillations in the trading price of the stock or the volume in which the stock is exchanged. While fundamental investors and traders hunt specifically for "intrinsic value," technical analysis relies on the exploration of price data trends and trading signals. Generally, they make use of analytical chart tools to assess the potentials of a given stock. This chapter will walk you through on all that you need to know about technical analysis.

What is Technical Analysis?

Technical analysis is a trading practice used to analyze investment and locate trading opportunities by examining statistical trends extracted from trading activities, such as the volume and movements of the price. Unlike fundamental analysts that tend to analyze the intrinsic value of a stock, technical analysts rely on market changes trends, trading indicators, and a myriad of other analytical chart instruments to measure the relative strength of a stock.

Technical analysis can be used for any security with historical trading records. It literally covers stocks bonds, options, commodities, fixed income, currencies, and other securities. But of course, we will be focusing on stocks, since that is our primary area of interest. Nevertheless, keep in mind that this analytical approach can be applied to other security as well. In other words, Technical analyst gurus believe that historic trading practices and adjustments in security rates can serve as a useful measure of potential price fluctuations in stock. You can decide to use technical analysis without having to apply other analytical cracks, or sometimes, it can be used in conjunction with some principles of fundamental value criteria. Still, in most cases, their opinions are solely dependent on the analytical display of stock charts.

Assumptions of Technical Analysis

We already know that the most common approaches used to analyze the performance of a given stock are through fundamental and technical analysis.

While fundamental analysis encompasses an analysis of a corporation's income statements to evaluate the market valuation of a corporation, on the other hand, technical analysis suggests that a given stock price already mirrors all information accessible to the general public. Instead, it focuses more on the analytical display of price changes, either in an upward or a downward trend. The technical analysis seeks to explain the market volatility backing the volatile movement of price by making observations, trends, and patterns rather than evaluating the foundational traits of a stock.

Charles Dow has published several publications on the principle of technical analysis. His articles contained specific underlying assumptions that proceeded to establish the foundation for trading in technical analysis. According to him, Markets are usually 'efficient with values' that reflect factors that are often known to influence the price of a security. Still, market price fluctuations are not probabilistic but adjust to known patterns and trends that appear to replicate within a given period.

The Efficient Market Hypothesis (EMH) implies that the market price of a security at specific periods effectively depicts all information available and therefore demonstrates the actual fair value of a security. This theory is built on the notion that the market price of stocks represents the absolute idea of all investors or market players, including institutional investors, traders, and other types of investors. While this notion is widely thought to be correct, it may be influenced by certain security report that may lead to both short and long term impacts on security prices. Technical analysis operates effectively only if the markets are less effective.

Another assumption underlying the technical analysis is based on the idea that price movements are not probabilistic in nature. It leads technical analysts to assume that trends, both short-term and long-term, can be established, which enables investors or traders to benefit from an investment based on the technical evaluation.

Well, we are basically far from the above listed. In this present day, we can easily conclude that technical analysis is strictly based on these three principal premises:

Market Discount: Most analysts barely utilize technical analysis since it only addresses price fluctuations and neglects other fundamental factors that we've discussed in the fundamental analysis chapter. Technical experts believe that all information spanning through the economics of a business to general market indicators and market perception is already on the stock market. This eliminates the importance of having to consider these factors independently before an investment decision is carried out. In this case, the only option left is the study of price swings, fluctuations, or volatility, which professional experts find to be the manifestation of demand and supply for several stocks on the market.

The Essence of Historical Trends: Technical analyst believes in the importance of historical trends. According to them, history patterns tend to replicate periodically. The recurring essence of these price fluctuations is often linked to the term 'market psychology', which appears to be consistent, and built on a series of emotions such as anxiety or curiosity.

They make use of various stock charts to examine these feelings and corresponding market fluctuations and changes to understand the dynamics of trends fully. Although many forms of technical evaluation have since existed for more than a century, they are still assumed to be vital since they explain the changes in price directions that are known to reoccur over time.

Price movement: Technical analysts believe that prices move, and in most cases, they shift in the short, medium, and long term. In other words, stock prices are more likely to continue in the past than to move erratically. Most of the technical trading strategies are based on this premise.

Exploring the Procedures

The technical analysis seeks to predict price movements of practically any exchangeable securities that are mainly susceptible to the interplay of demand and supply. In essence, a lot of investors view technical analysis as mainly studying the market forces of demand and supply, as expressed in the market price changes of stocks. Technical analysis is widely applied to price movements, yet some traders evaluate other variables other than prices, including trading volumes.

Within the stock market industry, a vast number of stock market signals and patterns have been produced by experts to promote trade in technical analysis. Technical traders have also introduced several trading tools to assist in making rational predictions and beneficial moves on price changes. Many of these tools and metrics focus exclusively on defining the actual market, like support and resistance lines. In contrast, others concentrate on evaluating the intensity of the trend and the probability of its sustainability. Some of these popularly used indicators and chart analysis include trends, moving averages (MA), and of course, momentum indicators. However, it is also important to note that these indicators may apply only to specific circumstances, industries, or classification (for example, stocks within a specific range of market capitalization)

Technical Analysis vs. Fundamental Analysis

Technical analysis and Fundamental analysis are two predominant approaches commonly used by market participants when investing in the stock market. However, these two approaches are contradictory. These approaches are commonly used when analyzing and predicting future movements in the price of a stock, and like every other investment theory, they have their supporters and their opponents.

Fundamental approaches to stock investment involve security analyses. Here, the inherent value of a given stock is ascertained to ensure the right course of action. These Fundamental analysts research all essentials ranging from the dynamics of the entire economy, the condition of the proposed industry, the financial status, and the overall management of a corporation. Hence, variables like company Earnings, investments, organization resources, and liabilities are all key characteristics of these analyses.

Technical analysis varies significantly from fundamental analysis such that the price and volume of stock are the primary inputs when carrying out an analysis of a given stock. The underlying assumption here is that most fundamentals are price-based; therefore, it is pointless to pay special attention to other variables. Technical traders barely quantify the inherent value of the inventory; rather, they make use market charts to recognize market directions that indicate the potential changes of these stocks.

Just like every other approach, technical analysis has some downsides as well. However, the criticism of this approach stems from the Efficient Market Hypothesis (EMH). According to this theory, the market price always reflects all the historical and current information available.

There is still no way to keep track of stock movements by patterns or mispricing. EHM economists believe history does not replicate itself, but rather that stock prices shift on a random basis.

More than this, technical analysis barely works for all categories of stocks. For example, technical traders may position a stop-loss order based on a 200-day moving average for a specific company. Furthermore, if all stock traders observe this phenomenon, the stock will hit this price, and a vast number of selling orders will still affect the price. It forces the stock price down, such that technical analysis becomes a self-fulfilling hypothesis.

Statistics may appear difficult to many, but they are the foundation of every technical analysis. By studying specific market data, you can see historical returns, trade volumes, and stock prices. Whereas the fundamental analysis focuses more on the long-term value of a given stock, the technical analysis of a stock is more focused on evaluating performance-based trends.

However, if you had like to analyze data and take a more active investment and trading approaches, like momentum trading and intraday investment, then you may need to take a deeper dive into technical analysis in comparison to fundamental analysis. Consequently, technical analysis uses various charts and may identify prospects to buy or sell a stock before the trend becomes too prevalent. Don't get me wrong; this does not neglect the importance of fundamental analysis in momentum trading and security trading as a whole. In fact, smart traders also take a critical look at fundamental factors of a stock when trading. These are often good indicators that can be used to back up a new pattern that is emerging based on technical data.

Chapter Ten: Getting a Grip on Technical Analysis with Stock Charts and Data

If you're going to become an active stock or momentum trader, then I bet you need a deep insight on how to read a stock chart. Ordinarily, investors, who solely use fundamental analysis to select high performing stocks, often use technical analysis of stock price volatility and movements to assess the precise buy or entry and sale or exit points of a stock. These essentially point out the importance of stock charts in general stock trading and investment decisions

Surprisingly, these charts are freely accessible on various sites like Google Finance and Yahoo Finance.

And on the other hand, various stock brokerages have continuously ensured that stock charts are readily available for their clients. But as funny as this may sound, while the information is readily available for most traders and investors, the vast majority of traders barely have information on how these data and charts can be used effectively to their own advantage. Well, this should be our main focus in this chapter. In short, 8

You are not expected to have any issue when reviewing stock after you must have studied the details of this chapter.

Exploring the Basics of a Stock Chart

Gaining a deep insight into the essentials of stock charts and data is a necessary skill that is required to study the overall performance of a given stock. It is also an essential tool to determine the general happenings of a stock market and how the stock is expected to perform in the future. Understanding these fundamentals can enable investors to make more informed decisions about a particular investment

What exactly makes up a Stock Chart?

The first thing you should understand about stock charts is that they have a story to tell.

It essentially explains if a given stock is purchased aggressively by mutual fund managers and other large investors, or if these so-called institutional investors are willing to sell out some shares as soon as they can. The second thing you need to understand about charts is that if you don't use them, you're basically investing with a blindfold on. Hence, you may not have a deep insight into what is going on with the market. A stock trader with no basic knowledge of a stock chart can be likened to a doctor without a stereoscope

In essence, we can easily describe a stock chart as a graphical display of essential information regarding the stock of a specific company. It provides information on price movements, current trading prices, historical lows and highs, shareholder dividends, market cap, and other financial details of a company. These charts come in the form of bar charts, line charts, point and figure charts, and above all candle stocks.

Using the NASDAQ composite as a key reference point, the following are some key components that you may likely see when reading stock charts; I will explain these components and what they mean when it comes to reading a stock chart.

The X and Y-Axis of a Chart: The x-axis of the stock chart is simply used to depict the time variable. You're going back in time when you move towards the left of the x-axis. Based on the time frame, every marker on the x-axis can be used to reflect ticks, minutes, days, months, or years. This just comes down to your personal point of view. The Y-axis, on the other hand, is where every price movement in the market is plotted on the graph. If you think about this carefully, you can see that the idea of y and x-axis is somewhat close to what you might have learned in middle school regarding how you can locate the slope of the line in the simple algebra class.

Chart Ticker Symbol: a stock ticker symbol is the most commonly used component in a chart. The symbol can to clearly define a given stock. In other words, it is used to distinguish a given stock from the other in a stock market exchange. For instance, Apple's ticker in a given stock exchange is specified as (AAPL) - see NASDAQ report, and Snap chat's ticker is specified as (SNAP)-see NYSE report. The ticker can be easily located under the section labeled "ticker," and in certain cases, they are located close to the stock name being used, specified in parentheses.

Furthermore, whereas some tickers appear exactly like the corporation name, not all corporation tickers are specified in like manner, so ensure sure you're not looking for the wrong company when looking for tickers.

The 52 Week High and Low Metric: The 52-week high and low is an important indicator that can be used to examine the stock trend over a specified period (usually an annual basis in this case). The 52-week high and low prices depict the maximum and minimum prices at which the stock exchanged during this period, even though they barely reflect the trading price of the previous day.

Moving Averages – Moving Averages are a method of technical analysis that can be used to define support and resistance on a stock chart. This can be grouped into 200-day moving averages and 50-day moving averages. In some cases, the red line is used to define the 200-day moving average, while a blue line is used to define a 50 day moving.

Volume – this is essential as it seeks to assess market momentum. Every bar depicts one day, while the line flowing through the tops is the average price over the last x- number of days. Thus, the higher the volume bar, the higher the shares of the stock will be exchanged.

Summary Key: the summary key is simply used to depict the important numbers from the stocks we are viewing.

An Open and Close Price: the opening price of a stock is the price at which a given stock resumed a trading session. The closing price, on the other hand, is more worthy of attention than its opening price for a given stock. The close price of a given stock is the price a stock ceases trading within the usual trading periods (after-hour trading may also affect the stock price). If the stock closes just above the preceding one, it is termed an upward motion for the stock in question (and can affect some factors like candlestick charts, which we will explore later as we proceed). On the other hand, if the close price of the stock moves below the closing price of the preceding day, the stock would show a downtrend.

The Relative Strength Line: The relative strength line evaluates the price performance of the stock to that of the overall market, typically as calculated by the S&P 500. Furthermore, if the trader wishes, a contrast may be made with another stock or index. This can be easily evaluated using its two technical tools; the support and the resistance lines (see next section for details).

Reading a Stock Chart

The stock chart is slightly different from the major information on the stock. Generally, the stock charts contain maps and line diagrams that reflect the price action of stocks. Although one can easily modify how the map is displayed, the price bars are basically depicted in bars, lines, or a mountain chart format. The slim line is often used to depict price swings or changes over a specific time frame, usually six months or a year. When using an interactive map, you can easily adjust the chart to various periods, spanning through one day to several years. However, when reading a stock chart, you must take note of the following:

Observe the Price and Time Axes: Every stock chart contains the price axis and the time axis. The horizontal (or lower) axis displays the duration you have chosen in your stock chart. This can be strictly modified, as it can be adjusted to represent anything from a time of year (or even multiple years) to a day.

Study the Trend Line: This may appear pretty simple, yet a fair chunk of detail from the stock chart can be seen in the trend line. Depending on the chart type and pattern, you can select various chart types, including the typical line graph, mountain, bar charts, and most importantly, candlestick.

- ☐ Line charts essentially display the price directions and volatility of the stock. This can be done using the last price of the stock.

- ☐ The bar chart takes note of the highest and lowest prices, usually daily. This, in addition to the closing price of the stock, is used to demonstrate the trend.

- ☐ Candlestick charts look slightly complicated when compared to the rest. They use clear or green boxes to depict various periods when the price of the stock is bullish (the price is closed higher) and red or pink boxes when the stock is bearish (when the stock price is closed lower) in nature than the previous day. The Candlestick Chart makes use of high, low, open, and close stock prices to chart patterns. For candlestick charts, you can use open and close prices to decide an upward and a downward trend for a stock. The candlestick also has a wide part, often regarded as the 'real body' part; this real body is used to depict the price bracket between the opening and closing of a given day's trading. When the "real body" appears full or black, it implies that the close body is significantly smaller than the open body. On the other hand, if the body appears empty or white, the reverse is the case. In other words, it signifies a higher trade close than the open.

Watch Out for the Trading Volume: The volume of a stock is usually indicated on the lowest part of the stock chart in green and red bars (or sometimes blue or purple bars). The important factor to look out for when analyzing the volume of trading is the fluctuations in the volume of trading, which can simply explain the intensity of the pattern-whether the high trading volume indicates an uptrend or a downtrend. If the price of the stock falls, the volume of trading is high; it can mean that there is momentum to the downward trend of the stock as opposed to a momentary blip (and vice versa if the price moves upwards).

Evaluate Support and Resistance Lines: Also, the support and resistance lines of stock are another important factor that should be studied on the stock chart. When a stock is traded in an uptrend or downtrend, it tends to fall within the so-called support and resistance lines. Ultimately, the support line is defined as the level that a stock does not fall below - in its simple meaning, it supports, pushes, and maintains the stock upward and prevents it from falling beyond that price due to market signals. Conversely, the resistance line is a certain point that the stock usually does not trade above; it resists the stocks that are pushing through that top price. Stock prices usually move within these resistance lines and support lines. However, when a stock price pushes through a resistance line, the initial resistance line becomes the stock's current support line, and the stock may as well rise from there. The reverse is the case as well when the stock falls below the support line. The support and resistance line of a stock is commonly referred to as the pivot point by most traders.

For further learning and visual chart reading for momentum, websites like investors.com offer most companies chart reading and fundamentals as a valuable resource.

However, it's is also essential that you monitor the movement of stock within the support and resistance, as they can be used to predict the overall trend of the stock and when it might go down or up.

Exploring Buy and Sell Signals

Buy & Sell signal system is a special trading strategy that prompts or directs stock traders and investors on when to buy and sell a given stock. As a pro momentum trader, a career that I have built with the last few years, I can't overemphasize the importance of the buy and sell signals enough. Well, if you have read this book from the beginning to this stage, you'd also agree with me that I like keeping things simple and simple doesn't depict unreliable or unprofitable. In fact, the simple buy and sell signals listed below should help you through your trading sessions.

Buy and Sell Signals and Recommendations

- ▢ **The 52 weeks highs/lows**: Examine and track the 52 weeks highs/lows to find high performing stocks. The 52-week highs and lows can be used to measure the highest and the lowest price a stock was traded in the previous year. The principle behind this strategy is that if price erupts from this range (either an uptrend or downtrend), there is enough momentum to continue the movement of price in this direction. The 52 weeks highs of a stock are usually based on the closing price of stocks or indexes, and vice versa for 52 weeks lows.

Assume XYZ stock trades at a high of $200 and a low of $175 per year. Then the 52-week high / low price of stock XYZ is $200/$175. Generally, $200 is deemed a level of resistance, while $175 is labeled a level of support. This implies that you can start selling the stock immediately if it gets to $200, whereas, you buy the stock once it hits $175.

▫ **Buy in an uptrend, sell in a downtrend**: in technical analysis, the directional movement of a stock is important. Here are one major investment principles that have kept me going throughout my years of momentum trading: Always keep up with the directional movement of a stock or, should I say, "*Trend is your buddy.*" The possibility of not sticking with a trend movement is equivalent to moving against the wind. Believe me, it's a bad idea. In simple terms, whenever a stock shows a continual uptrend or downtrend, you can conclude that there is a specific factor (for example, news and development) behind this persistent movement. In momentum trading, an "uptrend" is labeled "positive momentum," while a "downtrend" is "negative momentum." Ensure you buy a stock that is witnessing an uptrend over a long period, while you sell those experiencing a downtrend.

When trading in an uptrend, many techniques and strategies can be employed in analyzing these directional movements. You can choose to use price actions, technical indicators, or trend lines.

Some prevalent price action trading techniques that can be verified or nullified by more input from technical tools are to buy a stock when there's a price pullback during an uptrend, or when the price is trying to make a different uptrend. When an uptrend has two pullbacks (the moderate drop in a stock that occur within an uptrend), specifically after it is confirmed, and continue to trend, it depicts an entry signal. Most trend traders consider purchasing a stock during a pullback as a risky move, as there is speculation as to whether the price will spike again. Such traders recommend waiting for the price to rise again before they buy again. This indicates that they may end up buying a stock near the previous high swing, or when the stock moves to a super high region.

In the same way, you should sell a stock when the stock price makes a lower low.

Trading gurus avoids buying a high-performing stock after a major price drop. The drop usually continues further, and it may have reason to drop.

☐ **Use a basing period to find a buy position:** Basing is a general phenomenon after a stock has been in a long decline or the middle of a substantial increase. Stocks that are basing create consistent levels of support and resistance as bulls and bears battle for control. For experienced technical analysts, basing is important, particularly for stocks that have declined rapidly before a major turnaround can begin. Basing can also be seen as a "break that synchronizes," which encourages a stock to restart its bullish movement. When using a basing period to identify an entry point in a trending market, you should place a trade only if the price is higher than the consolidated area (when a stock neither revises nor rises).

173

- **Take advantage of a Weak Market Day**: A stock may witness a weak market day if it has few buyers and more sellers. These weak markets are often caused by market expectations, bandwagon effect, news, and major economic factors. Prudent momentum traders make immense profits by shuffling through various factors when a stock is witnessing a weak market day, while they look for strength during this period. Here is a quick example: you can buy a stock during a weak market day when you are certain that a stock will persistently witness an uptrend.

  A simple way to go about this is through in-depth research, fundamental analysis, and technical indicators.

- **Unique mix of fundamental and technical analysis**: Buy based on the unique mix of technical and fundamental analysis of your potential stock. In other words, you can choose a buy option if there is an increase in a company's ROE, earnings, and other essential fundamental analysis, which I have outlined in this book. You shouldn't stop there before making a move; make sure you apply your technical indicator as well.

On the other hand, don't sell your stock if you notice acceleration in both sales and earnings - hold your position.

Fundamental analysis uses a combination of quantitative measurements to measure the quality of a stock. In contrast, technical analysis makes use of share price patterns and trading volumes to evaluate when to buy or sell a stock. Nonetheless, your outcome can reflect greatly on your research and how well you've been able to study these stocks. It also focuses on how you decode the signals that have been outlined above. Note, the stock market may be volatile. Buying and selling signals are just two tools that you can use to stay ahead of market volatility.

Part Three

Putting Everything into Action

Chapter Eleven: Catching the Waves!

Evaluating stock market data can involve accessing varieties of information. What makes the information derived from fundamental and technical analysis more appealing is the ability to put everything into action.

Publicly traded companies are left with a vast amount of information and going through all this information, and some other variables may appear somewhat difficult to cover. At this point, if you had like to build a career in stock trading, you may need to figure out what your short term and long-term objectives are.

Obviously, the vast majority of this book is tailored towards momentum trading, regardless, evaluating yourself to determine the type of trader you are is quite essential for your long term success. So here is the question - Do you intend to invest for a long time, or you just want to make some quick bucks?

Your strategy will depend largely on your objectives; hence, the need for self-analysis before anything else.

Once you are sure of your goals and you've learned all the basic essentials as we have enlisted in this book, you can follow this real-world procedure to start *catching waves!*

Step 1: Examine Your Financial Capacity, Identify Your Trading Goals

It is important to examine your financial capacity and your goals before anything else. A person might have a great desire to plunge into the stock market, but if you don't have the money to make it happen, then nothing may materialize.

Here are a few questions to help you get started:

⬚   Do I have outstanding debt?

- ⍰ Do I have enough savings for my current keeping?

- ⍰ is my monthly revenue greater than my monthly expenditure⍰

- ⍰ Is your current monthly revenue more than a month's actual expenditure?

If you have a negative reply to any of the above-listed questions, you should take proper action to ensure you turn those to a positive response. The importance of your financial stand, when trading, can never be emphasized enough. In other words, the best time to invest in stock is when you have complete financial freedom.

When you've reached your optimal financial condition, you must take appropriate measures to ensure that you are clear on your trading goals as well. The following question should help do the magic

- ⍰ **The purpose**: do I intend trading stock for extra cash flow or future portfolio?

- **The amount**: how much do I intend to earn from my trading sessions?

- **Speed**: do I need quick returns or a gradual way to increase my savings?

You can make a quick list of all you intend to achieve. This should include both long term and short term goals once listed; you can arrange them according to their level of importance or urgency.

Step 2: Pick a Stock to Invest In

Since you're already familiar with stock trading essentials that have been covered in this book, you can now pick up a stock to invest in. More work will be done when choosing a stock to invest in. While you may find this boring, it is an essential procedure that should be taken to increase your returns on investment.

As a stock trader, I recommend you pay attention to finding the best-priced stocks. Even if you don't want to waste time shuffling through a series of information, remember that a poorly researched investment that has been resolved in a hurry will always do the portfolio more harm than good. Take your time, do the research now, and reap the benefits in the future. Trust me, the benefits will surely outweigh the stress. Adequate research of a given stock or an investment is the defense of an investor against incurring serious risks in the future.

To carry out adequate research about a stock value, find out the specific market place that offers the proposed stock of interest to trade. Take note of the symbol when doing this to avoid miscalculations. However, I advise you to research only those companies and industries that you are familiar with. Once you have chosen the industry of interest, compare key players, and stocks within the same industry. Check out their competition to choose the best option for your interest. And to do this effectively, this is where fundamental analysis of stocks comes into action. Just like we've explained earlier, a combination of the following analysis can be used to identify the value of a stock:

- ☐ Earnings per share

- ☐ Price to earnings ratio

- ☐ Dividend yield, etc. (see chapter 7 & 8)

Step 3: Set Up a Brokerage Account

There are several broker-free forms of investments that barely require an intermediary. In this case, you can invest in a given security without the need of a broker. Instead, you are only required to set up an online profile for easy access to your investment. Examples of such securities are ETF and index funds. Here, investors can easily access security by registering through their website, while funds are deposited.

On the contrary, if you want to buy stocks that require a broker, such as individual stocks or mutual funds, you will definitely need a broker service. Brokers offer various services to investors that may come up in some price ranges.

When choosing a broker or discount houses, ensure you take note of their inclusions of bundles, commission rates, and other maintenance charges.

Asides sorting out your transactions, brokers may also provide notable investment advice that can help you stay at the top of your game. For beginners, I recommend you use the Robinhood broker. The platform provides a cheap and easy way to invest in stock. That's right; it's quite an easy thing to do. The following steps can help you get started on any broker.

- Step 1: You can easily access a broker of your choice by visit the website or via app download. Most brokers offer a mobile app version for easy access.

- Step 2: Select the "Open Account" button

- Step 3: Create an Individual Brokerage Account" application for easy access.

☐ Step 4: Enter the necessary information, including your name, address, social security number, and date of birth.

☐ Step 5: Initiate the initial deposit by providing your bank details. Most brokers require a minimum deposit to be made. You can use a different bank account to initiate a deposit into the broker account.

☐ Step 6: Wait for confirmation. In some cases, the initial transaction may take a few days, while others may last for a week. After that, you may receive an email or phone call prompt informing you that you are all set to invest.

Step 4: Account Activation and Placing of Order

The step is the real buying phase of stock since you've got a broker, and you have funded your account, then you are good to go.

You can select your desired stocks using their trading platform by entering the company name or stock symbol you've carried out proper research on. Take note of the exchanges offering this stock. In other words, you can carry out necessary research to determine if your stocks of interest are traded in New York Stock Exchange (NYSE) or NASDAQ?

Review the price of the stock and specify the number of shares you intend to buy. In this stage, a lot of people make the error of mistaking a stock price for its number of shares.

Signal your broker to continue with the trade by setting the correct order form after completing the number of shares and verifying the total price for the transaction. Align yourself with the use of 'buy signals,' as explained in chapter ten, market order, stop order, and limit order. I personally recommend the use of limit orders as this often serves as the most active defense against risk. Once the order type has been set, click the submit button. Your decision to invest in a given stock has been successfully made.

Step 5: Planning Your Next Purchase

Buying a stock is a quick step towards becoming a pro trader. For every prolific trader, their major aim is to buy more securities while they diversify their portfolio. However, to get the best out of your investment, only invest and focus on 3-4 stocks; this way, you can keep track of your investment.

With this approach at heart, you can easily avoid the total loss of your portfolio, such that when one sinks, the high performing ones can easily take care of the loss. However, remember to work with the entry and exit strategies when trading.

A Quick Guide At A Glance

You can easily use the following guide as an entry and exit point using fundamental and technical analysis:

Fundamental Guide For Entry Point

Most pro traders combine the function of several fundamental analyses; some of them include:

- Start by identifying the market direction, check for profit, sales, and earnings growth.

- You can enter the market if EPS is greater than 18-20% of a quarter compared to the same quarter last year.

- Return of equity > 17% of (can be up to 25-50%)

Technical Guide For Entry Point

- Many high performing stock traders may get one or a few chances to enter the market when using technical analysis. The important thing to look out for is timing. Basically, the following should serve as a guide

☐ When there are higher highs. However, RS (relative strength) below 70 should be ignored, while a higher RS greater than 80 can serve as a good entry point.

Fundamental and Technical Guide For Exit Point

You should exit a trade if the following ensues:

- Lower lows

- When the stock price falls7-8% below your buying price

- Two consecutive quarter's deceleration.

Managing and Mitigating Investment Risk with Stop Loss

As a stock trader, you should never underestimate the importance of stop-loss orders on your trades. And except for volatility, the stop-loss shows you exactly how much you risk losing on a specific trade. Before you start implementing stop-loss orders to your trading sessions, you are expected to understand the overall practice of stop-loss, how to measure your stop-loss, and determine where your stop-loss orders will go.

Exploring the Essentials of Stop-Loss Order

A stop-loss order is a directive often placed in a broker to trade shares once they hit a given stock price. Such directives help reduce and mitigate the risk in a stock position a market participant may incur. However, if you place the stop-loss order at 15% just below the price you bought the stock, your loss will be restricted to a 15% loss on the initial investment.

For instance, an investor can place a stop-loss order for $21.25 if you buy the stock of Company Y for $25 per share. This will limit the deficit to 15 percent. But on the other hand, if the price of Company Y stock falls below $21.25, this simply means that the stock purchased will be sold at the current market price.

Stop-loss orders are often called "market orders," this simply means that it will take up any accessible price once the price has attained $21.25 (when the bid, request, or last price hits $21.25). Regardless, Stop order loss should not be reached if you notice any selling signals. They should be the last layer of protection.

The bottom line is this - if no trader is willing to take the shares off your hands at that price, you will probably wind up with a lower price than the price predicted. This is popularly known as slippage. However, as long as you trade high volume stocks or any other security, slippages during day trading is usually not a problem.

Placing your Stop-Loss

Determining the best position to place a stop-loss order simply involves targeting an acceptable risk level. This price and position should be determined strategically with a view of reducing your risk level. For instance, if a stock is bought at $50 and the stop-loss is set at $40, in this case, the stop-loss restricts downside trap to 20 percent of the initial position. If you're satisfied with the 20 percent limit placed on the stock, you can put a trailing stop-loss.

Stop-loss positioning theories are vast. In fact, technical traders are still searching for new ways to time the market, while setting stop-loss orders it is important to note that various stop or limit orders have different uses, which largely depend on the type of timing strategies that are used. Most of these theories use universal positions on all securities, such as 6 percent trailing stops. In contrast, some other theories use security or trend-specific positions like average true range percentage stops.

Another common method is the support method. This involves difficult stops at a given price. This method can be somewhat more difficult to practice when compared to other methods as it involves working out the stock's most recent level of support. You can put your stop-loss order well below that point immediately you have found this out.

The other approach to setting stop-loss is the common 'moving average method.' This method is quite easy to apply. Here, stop-losses are positioned below a moving average price for longer-term rather than shorter-term prices. Patient traders may consider using indicator stops that are completely based on large trend analysis. However, these indicators are usually used with technical indicators like the RSI.

Chapter Twelve: Exploring The Secret Strategies Of Experienced Momentum Traders

Quick fact – over 90% of traders lose a chunk of their investment when trading. A deeper insight: 60% of most traders quit the stock trading business within the first two years into the game. But the question is, what really makes the success for the 10% of traders who are still in the game? Truly, there is no magic way to go about this. However, the section outlines what and what not to do to stay at the top of your investment game.

The Rules of the Game

To become a stock market guru, you should dig deeper into your quest for knowledge. And truly, all you need is just a few minutes of daily reading before going all in to the trading game. These snacks of knowledge can appear like a diversion than any measurable tips. But here is the irony of the game; new traders are only interested in setting up charts so that they can start cashing out. But really, the whole game of investment is far from that. The following rule should help you stay at the top of your game.

Rule One: Adopt a Trading Plan

You remember the old saying: 'Failure to plan is a plan to fail' well, the same is applicable here. The idea is to choose a working trading plan that can help you stay at the top of your game.

A stock trading plan can simply be defined as documented procedures that depict the entry and exit strategy, as well as the fund management benchmark of an investor. The plan should be personal - although you can use someone else's plan as an outline, remember that every individual's response to risk differs. In other words, while some investors are risk-seeking investors, others are risk-averse.

It's easy to try out a trading idea and plan with the current technological advancement in the world of investment before you decide to risk real money. This technique is what most investors call back-testing. It compares trading strategy or plan to verifiable data, helps traders to assess whether a trading plan is feasible, and also reveals the probability of success when used. The trading plan can be applied to the real investment process once a plan has been established, and the back-testing depicts an incredible result. Nevertheless, remember to make good use of the plan. Even in cases where there seems to be a winning action, trading without following the actions of your stipulated plan is regarded as a deficient trading strategy. It may knock down any positive future projections that the plan may have.

Rule 2: Investment is a Business, Not An Act

To become a pro-trader, you must approach the investment game like a full-time business owner, rather than a mere act or a hobby. Trading should be regarded as a business, as it incurs expenses, profits, taxes, volatility, tension, and involves wide exposure to some type of loss. As an investor and trader, you are basically a business owner, and you have to do your homework and think strategically to optimize the value of your business.

Rule 3: Take Note of Technological Advances

Trading is a profitable business; it serves as a means of earning a large proportion of returns on investment, especially when done the right way. However, the game is a competitive one as more and more people lose out on investment daily. However, to earn a substantial amount from a given investment, you need to take advantage of the current technological advancement in the game investment.

Notable technological advancement has proven effective in the past. Charting platforms, for example, enable investors to analyze and examine an asset in an endless number of ways. More so, back-testing, which employs historical data for analysis to avoid incurring a loss, can act as a shock absorber from any unforeseen loss. Receiving market notifications with Smartphone enables everyone to track trades from practically any part of the world. Even the least technological advancement that we enjoy today, like easy Internet access, can boost the quality of your performance in a considerable amount. This explains the importance of technological advancement in a trading session. The bottom line is – you can use this technological advancement to your favor, while you relax and watch your portfolio grow.

Rule 4: Guard Your Capital

Saving funds to finance a trading account may take a considerable amount of time and energy. It may even appear nearly impossible when trying to save up again for the same purpose. It is worth noting that losing in a trading section is quite different from losing your trading capital. Every pro-traders has lost trades; don't fidget yet; that's an essential element of the game. However, guarding your capital involves taking zero risks, and pulling off all you can to protect your business.

Rule 5: 'Chew' On The Market

As a stock trader, you must educate yourself on the general happenings of the market. More than this, since various notions and subject matter contain triggering background information, it is crucial to bear in mind that understanding the subject matter and all its complexities is an evolving, ongoing phase; the same applies in stock market trading.

Continuous market research enables investors to learn basic market details like what the various economic reports say. Market research allows traders to develop insight and learn about necessary complexities in the market; this research is what allows traders to have a clear view of how those finance, economic, and business reports can affect the stocks that are traded in the stock exchange. In other words, the more traders are aware of common happenings in the market and the economy at large, the more informed they become in making investment decisions.

Rule 6: Invest Only What You Can Lose

Before you can start trading, it is crucial to ensure that the potential investment is genuinely dispensable. If it proves otherwise, you may need to level up your savings plan. It is important to note that the money in a trading account should never be earmarked for tuition, mortgage, or any other important household payment. Investors must never be left to believe that they are merely borrowing funds from the above-listed significant responsibilities. In fact, you should be ready to lose all the money earmarked for your trading sessions.

Going bankrupt is stressful enough; it becomes more disheartening when you lose the money that should never have been lost.

Rule 7: Diversify Your Portfolio

A quick tip – you need to key into diversification, as it protects investors from unforeseen market risks. Luckily the term is not as complicated as it sounds.

The term diversification is just a sophisticated way of saying, "don't put all eggs in one basket." It is one of the safest means of protecting your portfolio of investments against the many types of risk in the market. Diversifying your portfolio of stocks entails holding different classes of an asset just to mitigate or minimize risk (An asset class is a collection of identical assets.). Using this approach, a significant loss to any of the investment does not ruin the entire portfolio. More specifically, it helps you to retain some capital when there is some sort of loss in the future — and probably, to recover what you have lost.

Most investment analysts use correlation to make diversification decisions, measuring the degree of relationship between two or more variables. This indicates how to tow or more assets travel in the same direction on a stock chart and are often measured on a scale of -1 and 1. While −1 reflects perfectly inverse correlation, 1 depicts a perfect correlation between variables.

On the other hand, a zero (0) correlation between variables depicts zero relationships between variables, such that a rise or fall between two sectors and stock are unconnected. To diversify when trading stocks, you can easily do this by combining different market cap sizes, or you invest in various industry. That way, any market mishaps can easily be reduced.

Rule 8: Remember To Use a Stop-Loss

A stop loss is a fixed level of risk a short-term investor is prepared to take within each trading session. It can either be in the form of dollar value or a percentage on a given asset. In its simple term, it helps to reduce the risk of a trader within each trading session. Making use of a stop loss during your trading sessions can also help to reduce the emotions that are commonly linked to an investment.

It's a bad practice to disregard a stop loss when trading even though it results in a rewarding deal. Exiting with a stop loss, and making some loss isn't bad after all if it lies within the guidelines of the trading plan.

Rule 9: Quitting is Not a Strategy, But it Sure Occurs

Quitting shouldn't be a strategy anyways. But there are two reasons why most traders quit even after putting big money to work. A trader may quit trading because of an unreliable trading plan or, in most cases, when the trader isn't good in the game.

An unreliable trading plan incurs loss rather than the predicted returns in an investment. While there may be volatility in the market, or fluctuations in the instruments traded, when a trader incurs a loss from a trading session, a large proportion of the loss incurred can be linked to the trading plan. This is to show how important the trading plan is in stock trading. However, when a trading plan is no longer reliable, quitting the market isn't the answer. All you need to do is to re-evaluate the plan, and above all, make sure the plan is a SMART one (specific, measurable, achievable, realistic, and time-bound).

On the other hand, an unreliable trader is a trader that maps out a plan but either forgets or decides not to stick to it. Quite funny, you may say, but this is a major reason why most traders fail in the game. Improper time management, lack of funds, and poor planning habits can play a part in this issue as well. A trader that is not in the right state of mind either as a result of a health condition and some other unavoidable factor can decide to take a break. But like I said, quitting is not even a strategy; if it is a factor that can be controlled, you can easily fix such issues and resume your sessions. *Remember*, quitting is not a strategy!

Rule 10: Stay Focused

Remember to stay focused on the game.

An investor may lose on trade at some point, but what keeps 10% of investors that top the market daily is their ability to remain focused. In other words, we should not be surprised when we make a few losses — that is all part of the game. However, a profitable trade may just be one step ahead of the losses you incurred. The question is, how exactly do you intend to find that your earnings are only a few steps away when you give up?

More than this, you should never be alarmed by the few losses you incur as what counts more for every top investor is the accumulative earnings on an investment. When a trader embraces gains and financial depletion as an essential component of the game, emotional reactions will have a limited influence on the results of the trading. This does not mean that we can't be ecstatic about a notably profitable trade; instead, we need to remember that losses are never far away.

Hence, setting a realistic goal is a critical procedure for staying focused on the game. A trader with low capital should not anticipate a huge amount of ROI. In other words, 5% returns on $50, 000 is entirely different from 5% returns on $500, 000.

 In summary, talk is far from cheap when it comes to issues relating to stock investment. But then, you can easily stay at the top of your game if you can successfully apply the above-listed rules to your investment decisions. Hence, understanding the application and importance of each of these trading rules can go a long way in every trading process.

Conclusion

Although they may appear small to many, momentum trading in the stock market sure is big business. While millions of people are losing in the game, a lot of traders are also winning. What's more, a large proportion of people are trooping in and out of the market daily.

The broad appeal of this trading strategy is quite notable. In fact, whether you are a beginner trying to make money from the market, or you are a pro interested in taking advantage of market volatility, you will find that this trading strategy is really worth it after all.

The benefits of momentum trading are vast when compared to other trading strategies, but it isn't left without some risks and pitfalls. The good thing is that most of these risks and pitfalls can easily be avoided, especially if you've read the book '*catching waves*' from start to finish.

You can protect yourself even more by carrying out the fundamental analysis of any stock you are interested as discussed in this book. The good thing is that the strategies discussed in this book can also be applied to other trading techniques. This way, you are not only restrained to momentum trading technique.

More than this, if you have been misguided in the past by the popular investment phobia, the tactics provided in this book can help you get over it. This investment phobia can be explained by the number of losses where most investors traded a given stock at the wrong time, and with no proper trading guide. In contrast to this, other investors have been playing the game the right way, and I guess I can say that I'm one of them.

We've continuously earned from market fluctuations using the right strategy. You know what? This book can act as a market weapon to *crunch* the mishaps in the investment game, if and only if you stick to the strategies provided in this book. So, if you've read the entire book, you will see that you have been introduced to all essential concepts that are required to make you good at the game. From understanding the basics, choosing high performing stocks, to staying at the top of your game, we've essentially covered it all.

I began this book by exploring the three workable and friendly strategies (parts) to investing in momentum stocks, from these strategies, is where all other chapters of the book evolve. The first part of this book provided a strong base of understanding for readers. Here we explored essential concepts that will be beneficial when trading momentum.

Generally, the stock market is not where a novice trader can get soaked in the dynamics of the market. However, by understanding some of those concepts detailed in chapters 1, 2, 3, 4, and 5, you can easily understand the general essentials of the market. While chapters 1 through 5 explore essential key points that may appear a little basic, they are key factors that need to be learned thoroughly before any trading sessions.

The second part of the book goes further to explain how you can identify high performing stocks from a large number of stocks in the market. Here, I taught you how to shop for stocks while separating the good stocks from the bad ones. I explained how you could use fundamental and technical analysis for fishing for good stocks. While some folks have neglected the importance of fundamental analysis in the investment game, it is important to note that fundamental analysis sets the foundation in which every other trading strategy is carried out.

In chapter 7, I explained how fundamental analysis could be used to analyze the financial health and status of a corporation. Here, I explained how you could get a clear view of a company's performance using essential financial ratios. This allows you to perform valuable comparisons between companies in the same industry. The fundamental analysis goes even deeper to explain how you can determine the share structure of a corporation, and how you can dig deeper into almost everything that should be learned about a company's performance. With this, you can get a quick glimpse into its financial position and how it will perform over time.

Of course, finding a company with a good financial status doesn't guarantee winning the game, which is why it is also important to know the best time and price to buy a given stock. This is just exactly where the technical analysis covered in chapter nine of this book comes in. The various data outlined in this book can keep you at the top of your game - more specifically, when used in the right way.

In general, when the technical analysis is properly combined with fundamental analysis, the returns are vast. But one of the disturbing questions about the success of a trade or an investment is the fact that more and more people keep losing out in the game, even when fundamental and technical analysis are properly combined. This takes us further into to third and the final part of this book. The third part outlines how you can put every strategy and tip learned from chapter 1 to 10 into action. As evidenced from chapter 12, it also outlines why a lot of investors have loosed in the past, and why you too can also stay at the top of your game.

Hey, I want you to be safe out there, which is why I have taken time to explain some rules you should abide by to get the best when investing in momentum stocks and, in fact, any other type of security.

It is also important to note that reading this book from cover to cover is not the only commitment you need to become a stock market trader. What makes the strategies and tips outlined in this book work is the implementation of these strategies, and this can only be carried out by you.

The book essentially puts you in a winning edge, ahead of every new stock trader in the market. So here it is, *welcome to the big game of investment!*

The end… almost!

Reviews are not easy to come by.

As an independent author with a tiny marketing budget, I rely on readers, like you, to leave a short review on Amazon.

Even if it's just a sentence or two!

So if you enjoyed the book, please...

>> Scan here to leave a brief review on Amazon.

I am very appreciative for your review as it truly makes a difference.

Thank you from the bottom of my heart for purchasing this book and reading it to the end.

Bibliography

4 Ways to Diversify a Concentrated Stock Position. (2019, June 25). Retrieved February 7, 2020, from https://www.investopedia.com/articles/stocks/11/diversify-stock-position.asp

Cochrane, M. (2019, April 5). The Definitive Guide: How to Value a Stock. Retrieved February 4, 2020, from https://www.fool.com/investing/2018/05/13/the-definitive-guide-how-to-value-a-stock.aspx

Gala, P. (2015). *Momentum Trading: Trading In Stock Market*. Zaltbommel, Netherlands: Van Haren Publishing.

Kratter, M. R. (2019). *A Beginner's Guide to the Stock Market: Everything You Need to Start Making Money Today*. unknown: Independently published.

Larter, R. (2017). *How to Make Money on the Stock Exchange: The layperson's guide to successful investing* (1st ed.). Amsterdam, Netherlands: Amsterdam University Press.

WILLIAM J. O'NEIL (2009). How to Make Money in Stocks: A Winning System in Good Times or Bad (4th ed.). *New York, USA. McGraw-Hill Publishing.*

Learn How to Trade the Market in 5 Steps. (2019, July 5). Retrieved February 3, 2020, from https://www.investopedia.com/learn-how-to-trade-the-market-in-5-steps-4692230

Minervini, M. (2013). *Trade Like a Stock Market Wizard: How to Achieve Super Performance in Stocks in Any Market* (1st ed.). New York, United States: McGraw-Hill Education.

Mladjenovic, P. (2016a). *Stock Investing For Dummies (For Dummies (Business & Personal Finance))* (5th ed.). Retrieved from https://www.amazon.com

Mladjenovic, P. (2016b, March 26). Top Technical Indicators for Stock Investors. Retrieved February 7, 2020, from https://www.dummies.com/personal-finance/investing/stocks-trading/top-technical-indicators-for-stock-investors/

Nassar, D. S. (2005). *Foundational Analysis: Selecting Winning Stocks* (1st ed.). Hoboken, NJ, United States: Wiley.

Nguyen, J. (2019, June 25). 4 Ways to Diversify a Concentrated Stock Position. Retrieved February 7, 2020, from https://www.investopedia.com/articles/stocks/11/diversify-stock-position.asp

Nison, S. (2001). *Japanese Candlestick Charting Techniques, Second Edition* (2nd ed.). Upper Saddle River, NJ, United States: Prentice-Hall.

Rahadi, D. R., & Cakranegara, P. (2018). *Stage Analysis and Consumer Behavior that Doing Transaction Online*. Zaltbommel, Netherlands: Van Haren Publishing.

Slater, R. (1996). *Invest First, Investigate Later: And 23 Other Trading Secrets of George Soros, the Legendary Investor*. unknown: Irwin Professional Pub.

Stock Market - What is the Stock Market and How it Works. (2019, December 14). Retrieved February 3, 2020, from https://corporatefinanceinstitute.com/resources/knowledge/trading-investing/stock-market/

Wilder, W. J. (1978). *New Concepts in Technical Trading Systems*. unknown: Trend Research.

www.ingramcontent.com/pod-product-compliance
Lightning Source LLC
Chambersburg PA
CBHW030620220526
45463CB00004B/1355